D0471199

REVENGE
Redeemed

BOB STEWART

Fleming H. Revell Company
Tarrytown, New York

Scripture in this volume is from The King James Version of the Bible.

Library of Congress Cataloging-in-Publication Data
Stewart, Bob, date
    Revenge redeemed / Bob Stewart.
        p.   cm.
    ISBN 0-8007-1662-0
    1. Pigage, Tommy.   2. Alcoholics—United States—Biography.
3. Converts—United States—Biography.   4. Morris, Ted Martin.
5. Morris family.   6. Drunk driving—Case studies.   7. Alcoholics—
Rehabilitation—United States.   8. Forgiveness—Religious aspects—
Christianity.   I. Title.
BV4935.P54S74   1991
248.8'6'092—dc20
[B]   91-16317
                                                            CIP

Copyright © 1991 by Bob Stewart, Frank Morris, and Elizabeth Morris
Published by the Fleming H. Revell Company
Tarrytown, New York 10591
Printed in the United States of America

TO the memory of
Ted Martin Morris

Acknowledgments

Without the cooperation of a number of very special people, this book would not have been written. The principals involved in this true story have had to go back nearly a decade to recall this tragedy. Conversations and impressions of events have been reconstructed from these memories and are as accurate as memory allows. Written records and legal documents have been used where available.

My thanks to Judge Edwin White, probation officer Steve Tribble, former Hopkinsville police officer Bob Breathitt, Hopkinsville fire department EMTs Jerry Craft and Philip Keel, Dr. A. G. Campbell, Jr., Jim Adams, Larry Webb, and Plomer and Ruth Hunter. They helped to flesh out this dramatic story.

A special thanks to Judy Anderson for her rare ability to be frank about her family.

Upon meeting Tommy Pigage, it is difficult to collocate the soft-spoken, emotionally honest man that he is today with the alcoholic emotional cripple that he once was. Special recognition goes to his wife, Jacque, who saw the goodness in the man. The friendship of this Christian couple is to be cherished.

I want to thank Frank and Elizabeth Morris for opening their hearts to a total stranger and sharing their innermost thoughts. Now they are treasured friends. They are a Christian example; to say more would be redundant.

Finally I would like to thank my best friend and wife, Martha, who happily endures the gypsy life-style of a writer's wife.

—BOB STEWART

Contents

BOOK I
Death

Sunday
December 19, 1982

Trembling in shame Ruth Hunter awoke from her nightmare. The minister's wife had dreamed that young Ted Morris had been killed in an automobile accident. In her dream, she had barely taken note of the incident, showing uncharacteristic disinterest in the Morris family calamity.

The dream had been so horribly real that her inexplicably uncaring attitude toward the tragedy lay heavy on her conscience long after her pounding heart had shaken her awake. *It was only a dream,* she told herself, but she felt guilty, nonetheless.

Later that morning, as she described the dream to Ted's mother, Elizabeth Morris, Ruth felt tears tug at the corners of her eyes.

"I couldn't believe I dreamed that," she anxiously told her longtime friend prior to worship services at the Little River Church of Christ. "I didn't seem to care or be concerned, at least not enough. I didn't bring a meal or a covered dish or even come to comfort you."

Elizabeth patted her friend's arm. "It was only a dream," she comforted Ruth, silently alarmed at her friend's false guilt. "You would never do that to us. And besides," Elizabeth added, "let's pray that it never happens, because if it does, there'll be two funerals instead of one."

They both understood the undercurrent of truth and morbid humor in this often-heard line, but it lightened the moment. They hugged, then entered the church building to worship. That morning, each of them said a special prayer.

Tuesday
December 21, 1982

Tim Bass had already prowled most of the shops in the mall, searching for something special for his wife, when he spied Ted Morris, a teenage friend from church.

"Big crowd." Tim laughed.

"It's been like this since I got home from college," Ted acknowledged.

"Got anything in here Suzanne might like?" Tim asked, looking around the Sound Shop, a music store that specialized in records and tapes. Before Ted could answer, their conversation was interrupted by a beeper hanging from Tim's belt.

"Better run," Tim said, taking the beeper from his belt.

"You're in the ambulance?" Ted said, half question, half statement. His friend owned Bass Ambulance Service.

"Be prepared," Tim said, turning to leave.

"I'd like to ride with you sometime," Ted called out as Tim headed toward the door. "I'd like to see exactly what you do."

"Any time," Tim shot back over his shoulder before disappearing into the crowd.

Thursday
December 23, 1982

The shrill alarm brought Frank Morris out of a sound sleep at 6:00 A.M. He turned the alarm off, successfully fought the urge to catch a few more minutes of slumber, then rolled out of bed and padded to the window. It was still dark outside, the moon's soft light bathing his few acres in a golden glow. Frank never tired of that view. Frank hunted and fished with his son on this land, and the pair even darted over this wild terrain on motorcycles. This land was more than rocks and trees; it was home.

He remembered standing with his arms around his wife, Elizabeth, one spring evening after their home had been completed. He and their son, Ted, had spent the day working on the yard.

"This is it," he had told Elizabeth. "This is where we'll spend our old age together."

"And this is where our grandchildren will come to stay with us," Elizabeth had whispered, patting his hand.

Frank eased his yellow pickup truck onto the country lane shortly before 8:00 A.M., allowing a little more than forty minutes for the drive to the United Parcel Service office in Hopkinsville. Normally his 150-mile route would take eight hours, but it was the height of the holiday season, and that meant twelve-hour days.

Frank always relished the joyous holiday season. His parents and two brothers lived nearby, as did Elizabeth's parents, so it was easy to gather the clans, and this year would be no exception.

The father also relished having his son home for the holidays. It had only been three months since Ted had left home to attend David Lipscomb College in Nashville, and he had come home during Thanksgiving break, but for this close-knit family, the separation had seemed a short eternity.

Frank made a mental note to stop and see Ted at the mall when his own work was done. With his early schedule, Frank had been in bed most nights when Ted came in from work. He missed his son's companionship, but mostly he missed the nightly prayers the three of them used to share before retiring.

*   *.   *

At 6:30 A.M., Tommy Pigage fought his way to consciousness
through an alcohol-induced mental fog before he slapped the
alarm into submission. It was hard to decide which he needed
first, a beer, a cigarette, or an aspirin.

The hair of the dog that bit me, he thought as the beer won out.
He shook several empty cans on his nightstand before finding one
that still had a slight chill from the night before, mute testimony
that he had not slept long.

After a few swallows, his trembling hand shook a cigarette
free from its pack. The first few puffs provoked a coughing
spasm. Tommy's abused system rebelled, nausea building as
the cough racked his body. The coughing turned into a shallow
wheezing before he was able to suck clean air into his bela-
bored lungs. After another quick gulp of beer, the wheezing
cough began to settle and he could pull the smoke into his
lungs without rebellion. He pried the lid off a bottle of aspirin
and shook three into his mouth, drinking them down with several long pulls of beer.

That should take care of the headache.

But what about the rest of the day? his mind shot back.

That might be a little problem. He knew that a few hours of
manual labor on the tobacco docks would sweat the poison from
his system, and his fellow laborers were always more than willing to share a bottle. Besides, it was the Christmas season, and
liquor was plentiful.

He could make it. A couple of cool beers would keep his hands
steady until noon. Several more beers at lunch, perhaps even a
few slugs of whiskey during the afternoon, and he could make it
until he was back home and could get down to serious drinking.
Tommy preferred the privacy of his home when he drank. He did
not care for the distraction of noisy bars, nor did he care for the
people who frequented them.

Tommy, soft-spoken, almost shy by nature, had always been rather private about his drinking. He had sneaked his first mouthful of beer during his milk and Kool-Aid years, when he was five years old. He did not like it, so it was another three years before he tried another mouthful. Better, but nothing special. There were a few more mouthfuls spaced years apart, and it was not until he turned sixteen that he began to drink regularly, usually with a group of peers, and never at home. Voted most handsome by his schoolmates, the quiet young man was popular with his classmates at Hopkinsville High School, where he played fullback for the football team. He was a member of the Key Club.

The years after high school graduation were tempestuous, a steady slide into the depths of alcoholism. A semester at a local junior college was followed by a series of jobs, until finally, his tearful mother asked him to leave home because of his drinking.

To Judy Anderson, his mother, Tommy was just a young man full of high jinks who shirked any responsibility. She had never considered the implications of his drinking: that Tommy was an alcoholic. Mostly, she considered the aftermath of his drinking, not the root cause. Even when she demanded he leave home, she did not understand the depths of his problem. Actually, the petite blond beauty had never seen her youngest son drunk, although it had become commonplace for him to drink in front of her. Ultimately, she was forced to deal with the surly temper and unkind words that became increasingly more common each morning as her gentle son suffered from hangovers. She was always sound asleep when Tommy stumbled into the house, and the recriminations began when he awoke.

Once Tommy drove her to work at a beer distributorship.

Because of the nature of the business, a supply of beer was
kept cold in a refrigerator in the break room. She was alarmed
when he grabbed a cold beer at eight o'clock in the morning.
His habitual hangover had caused him to decline breakfast that
morning, but his stomach was not too upset for the potent
brew.

This is not normal, Judy thought as she watched him drink.
Fearing the public ruckus it might cause to call his hand, she kept
her silence.

*It's just not right for someone to drink that early in the morn-
ing,* she thought. However, her anger softened with the passing
hours, and she did not bring it up when she saw Tommy the next
morning.

Tommy's problems, coupled with other domestic crises forced
Judy to make a decision. Tommy had to leave! His antics had
caused enough heartbreaks.

The summer after graduation, Tommy had been too hung over
to take his ACT college-placement test. Once he had taken a
pickup truck that had a problem in an oil line and had driven it
until the engine seized from overheating. Another time he drove
a car into town without permission and without a driver's license.
One morning, the family awoke to the shrill buzz of smoke
alarms, to find the den ablaze. Tommy had dropped into a
drunken sleep, and a candle he had lighted had somehow ignited
a wooden table and a lamp.

Perhaps Tommy had been crying out for help, but his mother
had believed that he would not listen. Judy also found it difficult to discuss the subject with her son, so she took drastic
action.

"You're drinking too much," Judy Anderson had told
Tommy one September night as they sat on the porch of their

rambling home amid the tobacco fields six miles south of Hopkinsville. "And if we let you stay, it will just encourage your drinking.

"We don't want you to leave, but if we let you stay, we would be enablers," she said, using a term she'd picked up at a meeting of Al Anon, a self-help group for people who deal with alcoholics. "I don't approve of the way you're living, so you either change, or leave. You're messing up your life, and I have enough problems as it is," she concluded.

Judy had been fearful of her son's reaction. He had been a sweet-natured, almost shy child, who had turned into an inconsiderate, loud, overbearing lout who seemed to delight in using his tongue to inflict mental anguish.

He had surprised her that evening.

"I'll go," he said softly. *What am I going to do?* he had wondered. His stepfather's farm had been the only livelihood he had known.

What will become of this child? Judy wondered. It was a heartsick moment for her.

Now, three-and-one-half years after being asked to leave home, Tommy was back in Hopkinsville, working as a laborer at his stepfather's tobacco warehouse. For transportation he borrowed a big tan Buick used on the farm.

With a sigh, Tommy heaved himself out of bed and padded into the bathroom to splash water on his face. The image in the mirror was disheveled: his long blond hair hung limp, his bushy mustache bristled below bloodshot blue-green eyes, and his lean, muscular frame ached from hours of manual labor.

"You need another beer," he told his squinting image.

Ted Morris came bounding down the stairs in midmorning, ready to go to work. For the most part, Ted had taken life easy since he'd come home on December 8 for vacation, working afternoons and early evenings at the Sound Shop and hanging out with friends for a few hours each night. The money from the job would supplement a pair of scholarships he had earned to help with college expenses. In early October he was the only Kentuckian to receive one of seventy-five $1,000 scholarships sponsored by UPS.

With several weeks of college behind him, Ted had told Governor John Y. Brown, "I've learned fast that college is a lot different from high school. I have to continuously stay on my toes."

While Ted had good marks in high school—he graduated from Trigg County High School in the top 25 percent of his class—he had found college to be a special challenge. Generally his grades were good, with the exception of algebra. As in high school, he continued to struggle with that subject.

That morning, Ted looked around the family room. Like every room in the house, it bore a Christmas theme. Each table had an appropriate covering decorated with Santa Claus or Christmas trees or snow scenes. The fireplace mantel was embellished with a ceramic Santa and piled high with holly. Little nests of snowy villages, Christmas candy, and sleighs decorated lamp stands and coffee tables; Christmas posters proclaimed the joyous season.

"The house looks neat," he told his mother. "But it always does."

"Thank you." Elizabeth was busy crocheting a last-minute Christmas gift.

"Something for Gramma?"

"For our mail lady," she said, holding a crocheted collar up for him to see.

Ted cocked his head to one side to look at the work. "You've got a ways to go,'' he said, walking to the Christmas tree, where presents spilled onto the floor. "You should start earlier next year. It's almost Christmas Eve. It would be easier on you.''

"I know. You just can't seem to get everything done. No matter how early you start, there's always something at the last minute,'' she said a bit wearily.

Elizabeth the perfectionist, she thought. *Sometimes I make it hard on myself. But I love the results.* The house was picture perfect: clean, neat, but lived in. It was her job to make Ted and Frank comfortable, and sometimes her family said she went a bit too far. Frank had long since stopped trying to convince Elizabeth that his underwear did not need ironing. Nor did she have to stack it in a certain pattern in the drawer. Elizabeth's motto was simple. There was a place for everything, and if there was not, she would find a place for it.

Ted picked up a package. "Anything here for me?"

"Of course not," his mother teased.

Idly feeling the package, Ted continued, "I'm going to work late tonight.''

"Oh?"

"One of the guys wants off early, so I'm going to cover for him," he explained, putting the gift back under the tree. "Then Larry and I are going to hang out, maybe play a little pinball or something." Holding up another package, he teased, "How did that get under here? It doesn't have the right name.''

"I'm surprised anything's under there for you. I can't find anything under there with my name on it," she said. "Or at least anything shaped the right size.''

"Like a cookbook?"

"Maybe."

"Come on, Mom. You've been hinting for that cookbook for

a long time. Do you really think I'd do the obvious? I'd rather surprise you. Maybe Dad will get it for you." He tried to sound serious.

"I checked his gifts. None of them are the right size or weight," Elizabeth replied, playing the Christmas game.

"Maybe Santa Claus will be good to you." Ted paused before asking, "You been good this year?"

"The real question is have you?" his mom teased back.

Ted got up and slipped on his coat to leave. The movement broke Elizabeth's concentration. She looked up to see her son walking toward the door, his back to her. *What shirt does he have on?* she wondered. *It doesn't make any difference.* But for some reason, it did make a difference.

"Wait, Ted," she called out. "What shirt do you have on?" He paused, his back to her. She could hear him unzip the coat. *What's he doing?*

From the back she could see him gather his coat in front of him before wheeling and throwing the coat open in a parody of a flasher. "Ta da."

They both laughed, but Elizabeth noted that he was wearing a red, white, and blue plaid cotton shirt.

"I'm gone," Ted said over his shoulder as he opened the door and stepped outside.

"Wait, Son." Elizabeth hurried to the door. Ted stood outside the glass storm door. She put her hand on the cold glass, and from the outside he covered her hand with his, waiting.

"Be good."

Ted grinned at her, his dark brown eyes glinting in amusement as he mouthed the words, "I will."

"And be careful." Her standard warning in parting.

Again Ted grinned and mouthed the words, "I will."

His long-legged stride quickly took him across the yard. Elizabeth watched her son get into the small, bronze AMC Hornet, select a tape and slip it into the player, and pull forward onto the road before easing on the brakes for a final wave.

It was late afternoon before Frank found time to drop by the Pennyrile Mall. He and Ted had always enjoyed their time together. They relished their long talks, which romped through such diverse subjects as astronomy, politics, hunting and fishing, the progress of their beloved University of Kentucky basketball team, and religion. Religion was their favorite topic.

Some nights father and son would spend the evenings on their backs, spotting the constellations in the heavens. That idle activity would be interspersed with profound religious discussions.

"How could anyone doubt God's existence?" Ted would always say, looking at the stars, sparkling gobs of fire strewn against a backdrop of black velvet.

"That couldn't be an accident," his father would agree, his eyes roaming the skies.

Occasionally they would work up a sweat at the backyard basketball goal, where towering Ted would regularly defeat his dad in one-on-one. When they first started playing, Frank would slack off to let his adolescent son win a few games. Recently he suspected that it was beginning to be the other way around.

Ted was waiting on a customer when Frank entered. He waved a greeting, and Frank nodded. Stepping to one side, Frank looked at his son: six foot three, and still growing. Lean, with a slender face topped by a mass of dark brown hair with a slight curl, Ted weighed about 160 pounds.

"How's it going?" Frank asked when the customer walked away.

"We're busy," Ted said.

"It's that time of year."

"You should know."

A customer interrupted, and Frank stepped to one side while his son worked. *I'll just hang around for a little while,* he thought.

When the conversation resumed, Frank asked if Ted had purchased his mother's gift.

"I sure have," Ted laughed.

"The cookbook?"

"I don't think she even suspects that I have it." He chuckled.

Both Frank and Elizabeth had dropped hints for gifts that were inexpensive and within their son's budget.

Another customer, and Frank again stepped aside. He took pleasure in watching Ted work. Ever since childhood, Frank had striven to instill the work ethic in his son. Ted had helped his grandfather slop the hogs on his pig farm, driven a tractor on his Uncle Robert's nearby produce farm, and been a source of help on home-improvement projects. Ted had gotten this job his senior year in high school. It required that he worked Sunday afternoons, so he began to attend worship services at the Southside Church of Christ, not far from the mall. He barely had time to eat Sunday lunch with Elizabeth's parents before opening the store at one o'clock. His job was always waiting for him during school breaks.

"I even have a gift for you," Ted teased when the conversation resumed.

Frank suspected that it would be an eight-track tape of T. G. Shepherd's latest country hits, one of his favorite singers.

Another customer. "I'd better leave. You're busy," Frank said, turning to walk off.

"I'm going to work late, so I'll be home late," Ted told his father, then added as an afterthought, "Larry and I will be getting something to eat, maybe play a few video games. I'll see you later."

"Not me." A laughing Frank turned back to his son. "Tomorrow is Christmas Eve, our last big day. I'll be sawing logs when you get home."

"When you get older, you just have to go to bed earlier, get that extra sleep," Ted teased.

"I can still take you in a game of one-on-one." Frank grinned, challenging his son to a basketball game. "Maybe we can squeeze in a game tomorrow."

"Sounds good to me. I'll see you later," Ted said again.

Frank waved his hand over his shoulder as he walked away.

Frank would later realize that memories are made up of dozens of small events that are only half remembered, because nothing extraordinary marks their passage. But when subsequent events would cause certain memories to become extraordinary—simply because they existed—then unfortunately no amount of mental gymnastics would sharpen them; the moment would remain forever a lurking, half-forgotten recollection that sadly defied total recall. So it was that on this day, at this moment, it was simply a quick visit between father and son, nothing special to mark the event.

Slowly, Tommy Pigage straightened up from stacking tobacco leaves on the warehouse floor. He rubbed his back. The long day of physical labor had cleared his system of alcohol; he could see his hands beginning to tremble. He needed a drink, and he needed it right then.

Tommy willed himself to relax. He knew how to handle the tremors. A few good slugs of scalding whiskey, a cigarette to

calm the nerves, and the shakes would be over, his body returning to what had become a chemically induced normal. The tremors brought fear born in remembering. Only the week before, he
had run out of money. No money, no booze. No booze, no sleep,
only nights of trembling in a cold sweat under the covers, alter-
nately hot and cold, shaking until the bed became a thing alive.
The fear would become so extreme that he would find himself
praying, *God, help me through this, and I'll never take another
drink again*. It was a familiar pledge that always ended the next
day with the nearest drink.

These were hellish, nightmare evenings. Tommy would not
have recognized the words *delirium tremens*, but he certainly
lived out the acute symptoms.

Just be cool. A few more hours and you're home. Then he
could wrap himself in a chemical cocoon, with which he could
isolate himself from well-meaning friends who told him he drank
too much and from a mother who worried about his drinking. He
could enjoy the fiery explosion in his belly, the blissful serenity
when all was right with his world, no matter that it was through
a foggy haze that more and more lately had become riddled with
black holes.

Only a few months before returning to Hopkinsville, he had
begun blacking out for a few minutes, sometimes longer. He
suspected that it had happened occasionally in Lexington, where
he lived three years with Michael, a brother who attended the
University of Kentucky.

Tommy had been on a three-year binge of drugs and drinking
that had only been interrupted by sporadic financial reality. Three
times he had been fired from jobs. The first time, sloppy work
habits and drinking kept him from showing up for work. Another
time, he could not keep his hands off the merchandise in a wine-

and-cheese shop. The third time, his employer kept smelling alcohol on his breath.

By now, Tommy was occasionally experiencing double vision. If he were home, the double vision was of little consequence; but on the highways he often drove with a sweaty palm over one eye.

He and his mother had declared an uneasy truce, but Judy was too uncomfortable with Tommy living at home, so he rented an upstairs apartment on Canton Pike. His contact with his mother was limited, but cordial; she had loaned him her automobile for the Christmas holidays.

As soon as Tommy punched out on the time clock, he went straight to the liquor store. With a shaky hand, he took a large gulp from a bottle he had just purchased. The liquid burned all the way down as he felt the alcohol speed through his system. Soon his hands no longer shook. A second sip and his world started to take on a familiar happy haze.

After all, it's Christmas, he rationalized.

By eight o'clock, Tommy had drunk half the contents of the bottle, mixing it with water and ice. After a telephone chat with a girl he had been dating, it was decided he would join her at a friend's home on Donna Drive.

Tommy spruced up for the evening with a close shave, carefully combed hair, green plaid shirt, tan corduroy trousers, and a long overcoat to cut the December chill.

For just a fleeting instant, Tommy considered staying home as he studied himself in the mirror. *Naw. I can handle it,* he told himself.

Tommy drove several hundred yards west of his apartment on Canton Pike before crossing a railroad overpass that rises sharply, blocking the view of approaching vehicles. After crossing the bridge, he eased through a stop light and continued

west to Country Club Lane. It was only a few more blocks to
Donna Drive and his friends' home. Tommy drove with the ex-
aggerated caution of a drunk. Slow and easy, and no police
officer would notice him. Look how steady he drove. He could
handle his liquor.

The Morrises spent a quiet evening after a late dinner. They
half watched television as they talked and Elizabeth worked to
finish her handicraft.

An automobile buff, Frank had picked up a special-order set of
hubcaps for their Cadillac on his way home. The wire-spoke
covers gleamed in the kitchen.

"Ted's going to really like those," Elizabeth said.

"That's why I got them," Frank explained. He was eager to
show them to his son. "We'll put them on tomorrow."

The day's long hours finally took their toll on Frank. "I'm
going to turn in early."

Elizabeth nodded her agreement. "Tomorrow's the last day of
the big rush. And it's Christmas Eve."

A good-night kiss, and Frank paused at the door, watching his
wife at her work. "You should start that a little earlier next
year," he suggested, a bit concerned.

"That's what Ted said," she answered, amused.

Like father, like son, she thought.

Frank chuckled at the thought that both of them had suggested
the same thing. "Good night."

"Good night. I'll be to bed a little later," she said as he
disappeared through the door.

You mean when Ted comes in, Frank thought.

He had never known her to go to bed before Ted came home.

*   *   *

As Tommy pulled onto Canton Pike, Larry Webb, seventeen, was leaving his job at Kroger's grocery store to drive down Fort Campbell Boulevard to meet Ted at the Sound Shop. They had been buddies for several years, although they attended different high schools. Larry and Ted had met at a church party, and theirs was a typical teenage friendship. The two kindred spirits would while away the hours tossing a ski ball or shooting pool or planning their future; Ted had decided to major in business administration, and Larry knew he wanted to be in science, perhaps as a doctor. Often they would sink into religious discussions. Sometimes they went to the arcade, where they played video games; basketball was a favorite with both. A whiz at math and science, Larry routinely helped Ted with his algebra.

"Hey, man, my books are on the backseat, look where I've got the page marked. What does that mean?" was a common greeting when Ted picked him up. Larry would carefully work the problem, explaining each step, but the formulas never seemed to stick with Ted. He always needed more help, and since he came to work straight from school, he always had his books with him.

But there was no homework that night when Larry walked into the Sound Shop. The employees had just finished closing out.

Larry joined Ted in his evening ritual of escorting assistant manager Karen Bonner to her car.

"No," Ted cried in mock horror as they approached her automobile.

"Do you see that, Larry? Look how close she parked to my car," Ted continued, teasing.

"You be careful when you get in. I don't want you to ding my car," he added.

"You say that every night," she shot back, playing the game.
"I'm going to hit it good when I open the door."

"Not my car!"

By now the three were laughing, sharing the merriment.

"See you tomorrow," Ted waved as she pulled out.

Their conversation was filled with idle small talk as the two
boys took Ted's car to McDonald's, where Ted ordered a soda;
then it was back to the Family Hub, a recreation center across
from the mall, where they shot a few games of pool.

"Man, you ought to be a hustler," Larry teased his friend
after Ted won several games. Ted had sharpened his skills on
a pool table at home, where he even had his own personal pool
cue.

"Why don't you spend the night at the house?" Ted asked as
Larry racked up the balls.

"Sounds good to me."

"You can ride with me. There's no need to take your car to my
house, because I'll be coming back in to work tomorrow."

Larry nodded in agreement, concentrating on a shot. He
missed, wincing at how close he'd come. *I go to work at three
tomorrow afternoon, so that will work out,* Larry thought. *No.
Tomorrow's Christmas Eve. I come in early because the store is
going to close early.*

"It won't work," Larry told Ted. "I've got to go to work in
the morning."

"Maybe we can do it after Christmas," Ted suggested.

"Sounds good to me."

A couple of games of video basketball and the pair decided to
leave shortly before 10:00 P.M. Larry had called a girlfriend and
promised to call her back at 10:30 P.M.

Meanwhile, Larry wanted something to eat, so they decided to meet downtown at Ferrell's Restaurant, where he ordered two hamburgers and a small Coke. Ted munched on a Snickers candy bar while they waited on Larry's hamburgers.

"She's already got a ring in your nose."

"What?"

"Your girlfriend. She's already got you trained," Ted teased his buddy over the 10:30 o'clock telephone call.

Larry shook his head in amusement. Ted loved to gently tease his friends, and Larry knew this was something he was going to hear about for months to come.

"No, not me," Larry protested with a laugh, before countering with "You're just jealous."

"Not me!"

The pair bantered for a while before Larry sidetracked Ted onto college life. Ted was pleased with Lipscomb, especially the quality of people there.

"It's nice to be around Christians," he told Larry. "You don't have to keep your guard up as much. There's not as much pressure to do what you shouldn't."

He told Larry about LaJuana McDaniel, a special friend at Lipscomb.

"Girlfriend?"

"A special friend," Ted said. "Maybe my best friend there."

Ted had taken her to the airport the last day of school and was to pick her up January 2 at 10:13 that morning.

It was a quarter past ten when the hamburgers arrived, so they decided to leave. Since Larry was to call his girlfriend, the pair planned for Ted to call him at 10:35 and beep in; that way Larry would know he was home. The two friends planned to continue their evening visit by telephone.

"I'll talk to you later," Ted said with a wave as he got into his car.

The boys had parked their automobiles facing different directions, and each took the route his car faced when leaving the restaurant. Normally Larry would have pulled onto Canton Pike when he came to it, but that night he decided to take an alternate route home. He eased across Canton Pike, wondering if Ted would call him on time. Meanwhile, Ted pulled onto Canton Pike and turned west. It was as good a route as any, since he was going home from downtown, but it was not the normal way he would have gone home.

That evening had been a disaster for Tommy Pigage. He sat on the porch of his friend's home, the crisp December air keeping him conscious.

What's going on here? he wondered. The past hour or so was a blur of black holes and vague memories. There were mysterious tears in the knees of his pants and a vague recollection of falling.

He could hear a vacuum cleaner running inside the house, and that triggered a foggy memory of a spilled ashtray. That brought to mind a couple of puffs on a marijuana cigarette, but he could not put the pieces together.

Suddenly he was gripped by an acute sense of embarrassment tinctured with disgust. Although he could not remember everything, he was sure he had made a fool of himself.

Tommy's sense of embarrassment and disgust was made more acute by his drunken state; his alcohol-saturated brain demanded that he flee the scene of his mortification as he lurched across the porch and into the yard. Now he felt anger over some harsh words and sensed that he had succeeded in alienating everyone at the private party, including his girlfriend. To add insult to injury, he recalled that his host had taken his automobile keys, and it had taken a threat from Tommy before he got them back.

If they don't want me here, I sure don't want to be here, Tommy thought as he opened the car door. It took several tries to get the key in the ignition. A quick twist of the key, and the Buick roared to life. In a fit of anger and embarrassment, Tommy slammed the accelerator to the floor. The Buick shot onto Donna Drive, fishtailing the length of the block before turning onto Country Club Lane. A few blocks later, the Buick slid into a ditch near the intersection of Canton Pike.

Tommy gunned the automobile back and forth until it cleared the ditch, but instead of turning onto the pike, he pulled into a Minute Mart convenience store. His body had finally rebelled at the abuse it had suffered. Waves of nausea kicked him in the stomach; he fought to keep from passing out with each new surge.

All I want to do is get home, he thought.

He leaned his head against the steering wheel, struggling to maintain control, then put the car into gear and raced onto Canton Pike, dust and gravel spraying from under the back wheels. He was angry, embarrassed, disgusted, and ill. Perhaps his muddled brain reasoned that the faster he drove, the sooner he would reach the safety of his home.

The dispatcher at the Hopkinsville police department received a telephone complaint shortly after 10:00 P.M.

"There's a drunk driving east on Canton Pike," the caller had said, informing the dispatcher that the driver had run into a ditch before turning onto the pike from Country Club Lane.

Police officer Bob Breathitt, twenty-six, heard the radio call and pulled onto the pike, headed east. He knew he was behind the suspect, so he flipped on the patrol car's flashing lights and accelerated a bit. With a little luck he would catch up to him any minute.

In three years on the police force, Breathitt had seen mankind's foibles up close. But of all man's inhumanity to man, the crime of driving under the influence (DUI) seemed particularly heinous to him, because the very act of climbing into an automobile and driving in an alcoholic state shows a total disregard for human life.

Tommy Pigage's automobile tore down Canton Pike, his abused body as out of control as the vehicle he drove. He was only a few hundred yards from home when he drove onto the lip of the railroad overpass and passed out. The car sped on without his guidance.

Ted Morris was listening to a cassette as he passed Tommy Pigage's apartment and approached the overpass, traveling west. A rise at the bridge blocked the headlights of Tommy's careening automobile, which had pulled sharply to the left, directly into Ted's lane. Tommy lay slumped to one side as his car topped the rise and hurtled across the final few feet of the bridge in the left lane.

In the blink of an eye, before Ted could react, the 5,000-pound Buick rammed head-on into the 3,000-pound AMC Hornet. The larger car rode up on the front of the Hornet, jamming its undercarriage into the asphalt as it drove the lighter car backward. The force of the impact crumpled the Hornet's left front door jamb; the roof caved in; the steering wheel flew backward. The Hornet was hurled into a backward spin to the right, making a complete circle before flying across a curb onto a grassy area. The car bounced off the grass between curb and ditch and back onto the street, made another half circle, then hurdled the curb, coming to rest half on the grass, the front of the car pointing toward the opposite direction from the one in which Ted had been driving. It came to rest thirty-nine feet from the point of impact. An unconscious Ted lay barely alive, his body encompassed in a mass of mangled metal.

The Buick's left front fender was crushed as it, too, spun to the right, going into a sideways slide that ended in a three-quarter turn. It came to rest in the middle of the pike, eighty-seven feet from the point of impact.

The two vehicles faced each other, Ted's mangled Hornet bathed in the one still-functioning headlight of Tommy's car. The horrendous sound of tearing metal gave way to silence.

Only a few seconds later, Officer Breathitt came upon the scene. He backed his patrol car to the rise on the bridge so the emergency lights could be seen from both directions.

"You'd better get a couple of ambulances out here," he told the dispatcher on the radio. "I found the drunk driver."

The dispatcher noted the time and the date: 10:30 P.M., December 23, 1982.

If only I had been a few seconds sooner, Breathitt thought as he raced to Ted's crumbled car. Shredded glass and collapsed metal kept him from reaching through the windshield or the left front window. The officer had to rip a few shards of glass from the back side window and grope into the darkness to reach Ted, whose head was thrown backward on the seat. Breathitt could barely get his hand and arm into the hole. Blood caused his hand to slip several times as he tried to find a pulse in Ted's neck.

Careful, he warned himself, probing gently. A faint pulse in the carotid artery brought a surge of hope. *At least he's alive.* He gently patted the teen, a reassuring touch. "Help's on its way," he said, trying to keep his voice as steady as possible.

I've got to encourage him to fight, he thought.

"Just hang in there," he said, with authority and more assurance than he felt. "We'll get you out of there and to the hospital."

Breathitt heard gentle gurgling noises. "Don't try to talk," he quickly added. Then, not knowing what else to say, he added again, "Help's on the way."

The other victim! Breathitt ran to the Buick. He could see Tommy slumped over onto the passenger side. The door was locked, the windows rolled up.

"Hey," Breathitt shouted. "Wake up!"

Tommy did not stir.

Breathitt pounded on the roof of the car. He went to the passenger side, where he pounded again. "Wake up! Hey."

He studied the prone figure. He was breathing. There was a small amount of blood on the scalp.

Breathitt heard sirens. The accident had happened a few miles from a fire station and only a few blocks from Jennie Stuart Hospital. In three minutes, two ambulances and a fire truck were pulling onto the scene as additional police cars cordoned off the crash site.

Breathitt raced back to the Hornet, eased his arm into the twisted metal, and touched Ted. He wanted the boy to have the reassurance of a human touch. "Help is here," he told Ted. "Just hang on."

Firefighter EMT Philip Keel, thirty-six, ran toward the most mangled vehicle as soon as the ambulance came to a stop. It was as bad an accident as he had seen in his eight years on the fire department. He climbed onto the back of Ted's car and reached through the back windshield to check his pulse.

Good. It's strong. A flashlight illuminated the blood covering

Ted's face. Keel also saw that Ted was in a virtual metal straight-jacket. "We're going to need the jaws of life for this one," he told Breathitt. "What about the other one?"

"He's unconscious on the front seat," Bob answered. "My guess is he's passed out. I saw a little blood on his head."

Jaws-of-life firefighter EMT Jerry Craft, thirty-two, was on the second ambulance, which pulled up next to the Hornet.

The wreck stunned the veteran EMT expert. He had seen worse accidents, but never one this bad in the city limits, where slower speeds tended to curtail destruction. With Ted's car splayed on the curb and Tommy's at rest in the middle of the highway, it looked more like a high-speed crash on some lonely back road.

"You're needed here. I'll catch the other one," Philip said, heading down the road. "He's got a pulse."

Craft climbed onto the back of the car and checked Ted. The pulse was weak. He hurried to the front, where the frame had been shoved back under the automobile, and the dashboard and steering wheel were pushed back onto Ted. "Has he said anything?"

"No. I've just heard gurgling noises."

Internal injuries. Blood in the lungs? Jerry considered. *We can't worry too much about his legs. We've got to get him out of here and to the hospital.*

As Jerry checked the automobile, a pair of firemen used a crowbar to pry off the door on the passenger side. It was not enough to free Ted, but it was enough to allow the medical experts to see the rest of Ted's body and plan his rescue.

He's tall, so his legs must be broken up, Craft thought, dropping into a clinical analysis that required total concentration. *He has to be extremely critical, but he's still alive, and where there's life, there's hope.*

The car's frame was so badly damaged, he could not find a strong counterpoint on which to hook the chain-driven jaws of life.

We'll find something, he vowed.

If the machine could pull the steering wheel back, Craft believed there would be enough room to ease Ted out. He hooked one of the chains to the steering column. He took off his bulky coat, grabbed the other chain, and dropped to his knees, crawling as far under the wreckage as possible. He probed the undercarriage with his right hand until he found what he believed to be a stable portion of the automobile frame. He hardly noticed sharp pain in his wrist as he guided the other chain onto the frame, where he locked it in place. Easing out, he commanded, "Pull it apart."

The chains strained as the hydraulic pump started closing the metal jaws that pulled them in opposite directions, slowly moving the steering column away from Ted's chest.

"Easy. Easy," Jerry muttered to himself until the steering column gave and sprang away from Ted.

Carefully the men lifted Ted onto a long board, where he was strapped down to prevent further injury. Jerry Craft jumped into the ambulance with his patient.

"They're on their way." Breathitt told the dispatcher. It was 10:45 P.M., fifteen minutes from first report. Someone would later estimate it had taken seven minutes to remove Ted from the wreckage.

On the way to the hospital, Jerry's hand began to throb. *I cut my wrist,* he thought, vaguely remembering the sharp pain as he attached the chain under the Hornet. It took three stitches to close the wound.

*   *   *

Firefighter EMT Philip Keel had his hands full. After pounding on the window, he had finally roused Tommy from his drunken stupor.

Tommy unlocked the door. "What are you doing here?" he demanded, starting to get out of the car.

"Stay right there," Keel ordered.

"What for?"

"Don't you know?" Keel was amazed. "You've been in an accident. You might have internal injuries."

"The last thing I remember was driving my car." Tommy looked around, spotting Ted's demolished automobile. The mangled wreckage caused him to pause. "I was going home. Did that guy hit me?"

"Let me take your coat off, so I can get your blood pressure," Keel suggested.

Tommy cursed the fireman. "I don't need your help," he said, pulling away, bellicose. "I just want to go home."

"You can't go home until you've been checked" was the patient reply.

Keel knew there was a possibility that Tommy was uninjured. Many a drunk has survived horrendous collisions because the alcohol relaxed his body to such an extent that it flopped about like a rag doll. Since Tommy did not remember anything, he must have passed out.

Technicians arrived with a spine board. Tommy refused to be lashed to it.

His speech is normal, and he is responding to pain, but I've got to get this guy on the board, Keel thought. *He doesn't think there is anything wrong, but he has a head wound, and that could mean trouble.*

"Look, I'll hold you down myself if I have to," he told

Tommy. "You've got a head wound. What if it's serious? It could paralyze you, or even worse."

He paused, hoping this would soak into the befuddled mind. Something worked. A grumbling Tommy allowed the firemen to put him on the board.

It's going to be a long night with this guy, Keel thought as he boarded the ambulance with the troublesome, cursing drunk.

I wonder when Ted's going to call? Larry thought as he talked to his girlfriend. After thirty minutes or so, he decided that Ted must have forgotten.

Collective wisdom says that children should bury their parents and that even that sad milestone should come at the end of old age, after the family has shared many happy years together. Collective wisdom says it is the natural order of life.

Too often, though, young life hangs by a wispy thread in the emergency room of a hospital where dedicated people deal with death as a part of their daily lives. Although death is inevitable, somehow it is a bit easier to endure when it follows the natural order of life. When it stalks a child or a teenager—someone whose life is yet to be lived—it is especially heinous to a man like Dr. A. G. Campbell, Jr. He did not know how heartbreaking this particular case would become within the next few minutes.

Dr. Campbell quickly appraised his youthful patient. Ted was not breathing on his own when the EMTs wheeled him into the trauma treatment center. The emergency room doctor placed a hand-operated oxygen mask over the patient's face, forcing oxygen into his lungs, sustaining his life as the trauma team worked for the next twenty minutes to stabilize him.

How long ago had he stopped breathing? Dr. Campbell wondered. He saw the EMT. "How long . . . ," he began.

"He was breathing when we left," Jerry answered, spotting the oxygen mask. "It must have just happened."

Turmoil briefly interrupted Dr. Campbell's concentration as the EMTs brought in someone shouting obscenities and demanding to be left alone.

Within a matter of minutes, a ventilator breathed for Ted; chemicals pumped up his low blood pressure. Finally, Dr. Campbell could take a moment to analyze the situation.

Ted was in extremely poor condition. All signs pointed to severe brain-stem damage. The brain stem is the basic nerve center of the body, the hub of automatic responses that control body performance. X rays showed multiple fractures in the high spinal cord, where it entered the brain. Dr. Campbell could not help but wonder if the spinal cord had been partially severed; perhaps the brain had had a severe contusion. His practiced eye envisioned little hope.

The doctor carefully noted the symptoms and diagnosis on a medical chart. He had already decided to send the patient to Nashville.

The unconscious teenager had no response to painful stimuli. He was paralyzed. His pupils were fixed and dilated, a sign of oxygen starvation. His skin was cyanotic, or blue, another indication that the body lacked oxygen. Dr. Campbell circled *comatose* under level of consciousness and, on a scale of one to twelve, he wrote *three* under the Glasgow Coma Scale. There was a compound fracture of the lower left leg, the bone jutting from the skin. The patient had received a severe blow just above the left eye. Dr. Campbell circled "poor" under the heading of condition and felt he was being optimistic.

He decided to call the neurosurgeon at Baptist Hospital in Nashville. *Then I'll see if they can use any help with the drunk in the next bay. From the sound of it, he doesn't know what's going on.*

Elizabeth was still working on her handicraft when the telephone rang shortly before eleven o'clock.

I know, you're going to be late. She smiled as she picked up the telephone. Ted always called if something held him up or he changed his plans. "Hello."

"Is this the Frank Morris residence?"

"Yes."

"Is this the home of Ted Morris?"

"Yes." *Why would anyone ask that question?*

"Are you one of his parents?"

"Yes." *Why do they need to know where Ted lives, unless something has happened to him?*

"This is Jennie Stuart Hospital. There's been an accident. We need permission to treat Ted Morris."

"What's happened?" *O God, don't let it be serious.*

"Your son's been injured in an automobile accident. We need permission to treat him." Compassion mingled with the need to get on with business.

"How serious is it? Where's he hurt? Let me talk to the doctor." Normally soft-spoken, Elizabeth heard her voice rising with each sentence. It was the loneliest moment of her life as Elizabeth felt her hysteria begin to grow. How could Ted be hurt? He was with Larry. They were playing video games. He would come walking through the door any minute now. Only an insane person would play this kind of prank. But there was something about the woman's voice that demanded belief.

"First you need to give us permission to treat him."

"Yes . . . yes . . . do whatever you need to do. How is he? Is he critical?"

"We're doing everything we can. Please get down to the emergency room as fast as you can."

"But where's he hurt? Is he conscious? Is anything broken? What . . . ."

"Mrs. Morris. Mrs. Morris!" The stern tone brought Elizabeth to a stop.

"I have to go so the doctors can continue to treat your son. Please get here as soon as possible." There was an unmistakable urgency in the nurse's voice. "Good-bye." The line went dead.

"Thank you."

It could not have been more than a second, a blink of an eye, but that moment would forever be frozen into Elizabeth's mind. The telephone trembled in her hand, a combination of fear and the powerful jolt of adrenaline rushing through her body. One consuming thought permeated her: *Ted has been hurt! If he had been dead, they would have told me.*

But you didn't ask, her subconscious shot back.

They still would have told me, she reasoned.

For Elizabeth it was a fleeting time of contrasts, fast and slow, a state of mind that would only be revisited in the year to come in restless dreams. She watched the telephone as she threw it back onto its base, only it appeared to happen in slow motion. All the dread, all the portent of doom, all the worry that had kept her vigilant the nights Ted was out with friends, all these concerns came to bear in this one fleeting second. Had her worst nightmare come to pass?

Frank! He had to be told. He would know what to do. He would get them to the hospital.

"Frank! Frank!" Elizabeth ran toward their downstairs bedroom. "Frank! Ted's been hurt. He's been in an automobile accident."

Elizabeth's frantic screams immediately brought Frank from deep sleep to alert reality. "How bad is it?"

"I don't know, but they said to get there as soon as possible," Elizabeth said, grabbing the telephone. "Hurry, Frank. Hurry. We have to get to Ted." She was almost babbling in the intensity of the moment. "They wanted permission to treat him."

Frank began to pull on the clothes he had laid out for work the next morning.

"Hurry! We've got to get there," she urged, impatiently waiting for the telephone to be answered.

"Ruth. This is Elizabeth. Ted's been hurt in an accident. He's at Jennie Stuart Hospital. Would you and Plomer go on over to the hospital to do whatever you can? At least someone will be there. And Ruth, tell them we're on our way."

A fleeting thought. *That was dumb. I already told the hospital we were on our way.*

By now Frank was frantically running from dresser to chest of drawers to night stand. "Where are the car keys?"

Elizabeth grabbed her purse and started searching. "I have a set in my purse," she said, but before she could find them, Frank had located his keys on the night stand.

The two started to leave when Elizabeth grabbed Frank. He looked down into her large, frightened eyes; she was more vulnerable than he had ever seen her.

"Oh, Frank." A sob constricted her throat. "Pray, Frank. Just pray that our son will be all right."

Frank wrapped his wife in his arms, wishing he could protect her from this horrible moment. "Lord God. We're scared. We don't know what to expect. Protect our son. Keep him safe. You know how much we love him . . . ."

Emotion choked his words off. Elizabeth felt her husband shudder as he heaved a deep sigh, reaching down into the recesses of his very soul to pull himself together.

It would have been easier to give in to the emotions of the moment, to weep at the unknown, but with an almost superhuman effort, he whispered in conclusion: "In Jesus' name. Amen."

"Amen," Elizabeth whispered.

Hand in hand, the two hurried from the room. By the time they reached the den, they were trotting. Outside, they ran madly for their automobile. They had a sixteen-mile drive ahead of them.

As the Morrises drove into the hospital parking lot, Frank made a decision. "As soon as we go in, you stay with Plomer and Ruth," he said as they parked. "I'm going to find Ted."

Elizabeth nodded in agreement.

As they hurried down the slanted sidewalk, they spied Plomer and Ruth Hunter looking out the door for them.

"We don't know anything yet." Plomer answered the unspoken question as the Morrises burst into the emergency receiving room. "We've been here since a few minutes after Elizabeth called."

"Is he . . . ?"

"He's alive. We know that much," Plomer said. "They won't let anyone back there, even though I told them I was a minister."

A nurse instructed them all to go into the emergency waiting room.

"Where is he?"

"In there," Plomer said, indicating a pair of massive swinging doors bearing the legend, DO NOT ENTER.

In a heartbeat Frank crossed the waiting room and plunged through the doors into the controlled chaos and fear that mark emergency treatment areas. Curtains were drawn around several cubicles. He could hear people behind them.

A loud drunk was pushing helping hands aside. Frank paid him scant attention.

"Hey, you're not supposed to be back here," an orderly said when he saw Frank.

Screwing up his courage, Frank pulled a curtain aside. It was not Ted. The orderly started toward the distraught father as Frank pulled back another curtain. It was empty. He went to the third cubicle.

A nurse took Frank's arm before he pulled the curtain.

"You can't be back here," she said in a stern but gentle tone.

"Where is Ted Morris?" A demand.

The nurse nervously eyed the curtain in Frank's hand. "You shouldn't be back here," she said, motioning to the orderly who had joined them. "He'll show you the way out."

"I want to find my boy," Frank insisted.

"The doctors are doing everything they can. They'll be out shortly." She tried to soothe the agitated father.

Frank pulled free from her grip and yanked the curtain aside. He thought he was prepared, but he was not. Ted lay on a table, a tube disappearing down his throat. It was attached to a machine that pumped oxygen into his lungs and eased his breathing. Energy-producing glucose dripped down an intravenous tube into the veins of his right arm. Frank was so stunned that he did not see Dr. Campbell step back and silently signal the orderly to let Frank stay.

Frank Morris? Not Frank Morris. The realization jolted the physician. *This must be Frank Morris's son.* It's one thing to treat a total stranger, but still another to treat the child of a friend. The two had developed a friendship over the years as Frank delivered UPS packages to his office.

Dr. Campbell decided to remain quiet, to give the father a few moments alone. *Besides, I really don't know what to say.*

Frank felt rooted to the spot, his eyes riveted on Ted. *At least he's alive.* His son wore only his undershorts; the rest of his clothes had been stripped away. Frank tried to comprehend what he saw. Small nicks covered his legs and face. There was a puncture wound to his left side, a bandage was on the lower left leg, and another bandage covered what Frank assumed was a serious wound over his left eye. A brace held Ted's neck stiff.

Slowly Frank started to approach Ted. He was suffering a turbulent mixture of emotions. With each step, he felt as if someone were pushing him from the back and another person were pulling him from the front. He wanted—no, he *demanded,* to be there—but at the same time, he wished he were anywhere else in the world. Finally, a father's love overcame it all and he rushed forward, taking Ted's hand.

Now that he had found Ted, Frank did not know what to do. *Pray,* Elizabeth had told him. *Pray!*

And he did. Tears trickling down his cheeks, Frank begged God for his son's life. After silent seconds, he squeezed Ted's hand. "I'm here. You're going to be all right."

There was no response.

Frank reached down and opened Ted's unbandaged eye. It stared straight ahead, unmoving. "Son. Son." He gripped Ted's hand, wishing that his very touch could heal his son. "I love you."

"He can't hear you."

Startled, Frank turned to face Dr. Campbell.

"Sure, he can hear me."

"I'm sorry, Frank, but he can't," Dr. Campbell said with a

sigh, adding, "I wish he could. His neck's broken, and I suspect that there has been damage to the brain stem." He paused to let the information soak in.

"Can't you do something? Operate?" Frank said, more of a command than a question.

"He has a strong pulse, and that's good." Dr. Campbell paused. Now came the hard part. "He's in very poor condition," he added. Handling parents was routine, but this was more difficult than any he had ever encountered. Frank's eyes were almost glazed. *He's in mild shock,* Dr. Campbell warned himself. *Be careful.*

"He received a severe blow to the head. All the indicators point to brain damage," the doctor explained, adding that an ambulance was already on the way to take Ted to Nashville, where he would be treated by a neurosurgeon.

"But, Frank, I have to tell you that his chances are very small." Dr. Campbell's empathy almost overwhelmed him, a rare event for a man who must daily steel himself against calamity. "He's in very poor condition."

How do I tell her these things? Frank wondered when Elizabeth looked at him expectantly as he walked across the waiting room and knelt in front of her, taking her hands in his.

"He is alive." Those words should have comforted her, but Elizabeth could tell from Frank's face that there was much more. She waited fearfully. Unable to look his wife in the eyes, Frank added, "He is very critical." Another long pause. "The doctor says Ted has brain damage. He believes his best hope is to be treated by a neurosurgeon in Nashville. He's already called a doctor there and ordered an ambulance."

"But he's alive?"

"Yes."

"What did he look like?"

"Cuts, nicks, a blow to the head. But to look at him, it doesn't look that bad."

"Can I go see him?"

"I think it would be best if you didn't. They have him hooked up to a machine."

"A machine?"

"It's to help him breathe."

"Can't he breathe on his own?"

"I don't know." Find safer ground. "The doctor says his leg's broken."

"Which one?"

"I don't know." He paused, visualizing Ted on the bed. "His left, I think. He's got a puncture wound—that's what the doctor called it—on his left side."

She looked at him.

"And the doctor believes his neck is broken."

"Oh, Frank," Elizabeth sobbed as Ruth came over to help comfort her.

"We have to keep hope. He's alive. He can always recover," Frank emphasized.

While Frank was in with Ted, the Hunters' son, Jimmy, had driven to the wrecking-service storage yard and retrieved as many of Ted's belongings as he could find in the dark.

It was decided that they would all ride to Nashville in the Morris's car. Jimmy Hunter volunteered to drive. They would follow the ambulance, but before they left, Frank asked that they join hands and pray.

*   *   *

"Well, you really did it this time!"

Tommy Pigage looked up to see his stepfather, Phelps Anderson, standing in the emergency room. Dr. Campbell noticed that Phelps's presence seemed to have an immediate calming effect on the disoriented young man.

"You went and got yourself caught again," Phelps added with disgust.

"What happened?" Tommy asked, confused, the fear of the unknown tugging at his vague memories. It seemed to him that he had spent hours in the emergency room, and it also seemed to him that the medical team had ignored his needs. His head throbbed, his body ached, his mind was befuddled. But it was obvious, even in his current mental state, that he was in trouble.

"You don't know?" Phelps could hardly believe that Tommy did not remember what had happened only minutes earlier.

"The last thing I remember was driving home," Tommy answered.

"You were in a car accident." Phelps paused. When Tommy did not respond, Phelps added, "You know that you ran into somebody?"

Perhaps it was a simply a familiar face, or the fear of the unknown, or the adrenaline coursing through his veins at Phelps's words, but the seriousness of the situation finally began to cut through Tommy's alcohol-induced fog. Fear began to purge him of his bellicose demeanor.

What do I say? What do I do? His mind raced to consider the situation. Finally he asked, "Is he okay?"

"I'm told that the other boy is in very critical condition."

The ambulance team headed by Tim Bass interrupted the conversation as it hustled through the emergency room to disappear behind the curtains surrounding the treatment bay where Ted Morris lay fighting for his life. The men were silent as Dr. Campbell joined the team. They could hear the creaks of the gurney, the muffled conversations as Ted was prepared for the trip to Nashville.

Phelps searched the face of this young man who had been a son to him for more than a decade. "It's very serious," he said in answer to Tommy's question. "They say that he may not be all right."

All-consuming fear began to enfold Tommy, like a black cloak that wrapped itself around his shoulders and clamped itself to his very soul.

A commotion in the emergency-room hallway interrupted the waiting-room prayer. Tim Bass was pushing a gurney toward an outside door as his wife, Suzanne, trotted beside it, manually operating a ventilator bag. Dr. Campbell walked briskly behind.

Elizabeth looked up to catch a glimpse of her son as the trio disappeared out the door. A sheet covered him. All she saw was his tousled hair.

Dr. Campbell reappeared in a few seconds. "It's time."

The prayer ended, the group left. A nurse handed Elizabeth a small bag as she went out the door. "Your son's personal belongings," she said, gently reaching out to touch Elizabeth's arm. "Do you want his clothes?"

"No." Elizabeth turned to leave.

As Frank started out the door behind her, he turned to Dr. Campbell, who raised his hand in a farewell gesture that also portrayed his own frustration and fear.

He's really troubled that Ted is my son. "Thanks."

The doctor nodded. "They're waiting for you in Nashville."

Frank bolted through the door after the others. Dr. Campbell looked at the clock. It was midnight. Christmas Eve. It would be days before he would shake the depression that settled on him that night.

Friday
December 24, 1982

Tim Bass had to be dispassionate. To do otherwise would be self-destructive, since he had spent his life picking up the mangled bodies of acquaintances, sometimes of friends.

But on this night it was virtually impossible for him to control his anger and sorrow as he flipped on the emergency lights and gunned the ambulance out of the parking lot. He had seen the doctor's written report and was pessimistic. *I have a funeral I'm getting ready to go to.*

Tim was silent as he guided the ambulance through the deserted town and onto Interstate 24, where he eased down on the accelerator until the ambulance was cruising at nearly eighty miles per hour.

"How's he doing?" he called back to Suzanne, who patiently monitored Ted's vital signs.

"He hasn't changed."

Tim pushed the ambulance's speedometer up to eighty-five. "Did you see the guy who hit him? He was in the next room, cussing and drunk." Tim had a mental picture of Tommy: long hair matted with blood, voice raised in belligerence. "He didn't want anyone to help him. He was . . . ." Tim searched for just the right description. "Abusive . . . vulgar."

Suzanne had only a casual acquaintance with Ted, but she knew that he was one of her husband's church buddies.

I have a funeral I'm getting ready to go to.

Tim was frustrated by the injustice of it all. "Ted doesn't drink, smoke, or cuss. That I know," he told his wife. "He is more or less a perfect kid."

Suzanne remained quiet. Let him blow off steam.

"That drunk really screwed him up," Tim added.

Tommy's scalp had been sliced along both sides of his hairline, just above his forehead. It took several stitches to close the four-inch cuts. As they worked, Officer Breathitt arrived to ask for a blood sample.

No! was the first thought in Tommy's clearing mind. *They take a blood sample and they'll find alcohol.*

"How about it?" his stepfather asked.

But if I refuse, then it's like admitting guilt. "Ah . . . ." Tommy searched for a way out. *There is none.* "Ah. . . ." And finally on reluctant "Okay." *I might as well get ready to go to jail.*

Conversation was at a minimum as Jimmy Hunter tried unsuccessfully to keep up with the ambulance. Frank and Elizabeth huddled together in the backseat and bleakly watched the blinking lights disappear down the interstate. There was no use jeopardizing their lives by driving too fast.

As expected, Frank was very cool in the face of the difficulties, but from the first, Plomer and Ruth had been concerned about Elizabeth. Ted was an only child, and Elizabeth was very protective, very motherly. Her husband and son were the center of her universe, and should Ted die, they feared it might crush her. From what little information the group could gather, Plomer expected Ted to survive.

However, Plomer wrestled with an even greater fear than that of death. He believed it was a topic that should be considered. Perhaps it would even help prepare Elizabeth. Finally, he broke the silence. "You know, there could be things worse than death."

The thought stunned Elizabeth.

"Ted could survive this and be paralyzed," he said gently.

"I want him any way I can have him," Elizabeth replied.

"What if he survived this and he doesn't know anything?" he asked. "What if there is brain damage and he doesn't know you?"

"I still want him any way I can have him," she stressed.

"That could be worse than death," Plomer said gently, trying to prepare his friends for any eventuality.

Elizabeth took Ted's high-school class ring from the bag the nurse had handed her. She slipped it over her index finger and stared at it, slowly stroking it.

The seventy-mile drive to the hospital normally takes ninety minutes. Jimmy made it in an hour, even losing a few minutes trying to locate Baptist Hospital. Although frustrated at the delay, Frank could not help but notice a downtown building in which the office lights sent the message: PEACE ON EARTH.

They found Tim's ambulance backed up to the emergency entrance, the door still standing open. Inside, the nurse instructed them to be seated and wait.

It was a quiet ride to the Anderson home for Tommy. He had finally come to comprehend exactly what had happened. Shock became part of his all-encompassing fear. "Do you know the name of the boy I hit?"

"I think it was *Morris*." Phelps drove on in silence before adding, "His parents live off the road you had the wreck on."

Self-pity mingled with shame fueled Tommy's emotional turmoil.

This guy might die! That thought kept repeating itself over and over in Tommy's mind. He feared that he might go to jail. *What would happen to me there?* He had shamed his family's good name. *I did it again. I'm the black sheep. I'll never be any good to my family. I just wish I could move to a different world, just a different plane of existence, and leave all my troubles behind.*

It never occurred to him that he had already tried that through alcoholism.

Judy greeted her son at the door. "Hi, Tommy. How are you?"

"I'm just fine." *I'm not really, but why go into all that? She'd just get mad and we'd end up in a fight.* "I'm tired. I just want to hit the bed."

Judy nodded. She was too angry to talk.

What am I going to do now? Tommy wondered.

Ted had held his own during the ambulance ride, but his condition started to slip once he reached the hospital.

It was unusual for Tim to remain at a hospital after an emergency run, but he could not bring himself to walk away from Ted. Tim watched as Dr. Arthur Bond grimly examined his friend. Without being told so by the neurologist, Tim knew the end was near.

"I'll go alert his folks," Tim suggested. Dr. Bond nodded his agreement.

He's just not going to make it. Aloud, he told the surgeon, "I don't know what this is going to do to the Morrises. He's their only son, and they worship the ground he walks on."

It was a few seconds before Plomer looked up to see Tim standing in the hallway. Tim signaled for him. "I don't believe there is any way Ted will make it. There's too much damage to his head," Tim said. "I think you'd better prepare the family."

No sooner had Tim left than a nurse came into the waiting room to inform the parents that the doctors were preparing Ted for surgery. Instead of operating on his brain, the nurse said a pin would be inserted into his broken leg.

Plomer decided to keep Tim's information to himself. *Why cause more stress right now? Tim could be wrong. Why would they be operating on his leg if he were brain dead?*

"Maybe it's not as bad as we think," Frank told Elizabeth.

"Frank, maybe our prayers are being answered."

He squeezed her hand.

The minutes continued to tick past as they waited for more than an hour. Ted's parents and friends did not know that they were maintaining a death watch as minutes turned into an hour.

Tim and Suzanne resumed their vigil as Ted's vital signs continued to fall. Shortly after two o'clock, his heartbeat went awry. The two watched as the doctor and nurses struggled to regulate the heartbeat with chemicals before manually pumping the chest to keep the life-sustaining blood flowing. The heart stopped. Dr. Bond used electric defibrillators and more medicine in an attempt to start the heart again. The paddles sent fingers of electricity probing the organ for that one spot where life could be sparked. Powerful drugs intermingled with the electric stimulus, but mankind's knowledge could not rekindle Ted's life.

His battered body and courageous young heart could take no more.

As his parents prayed with other friends, Ted Martin Morris entered a new phase of eternity, to stand before his Creator.

BOOK II
Aftermath

Friday
December 24, 1982

Silence.

"I think you'd better go with me," Dr. Bond said. Tim Bass nodded. Turning to his nurse, the doctor continued. "Call the receptionist and tell her to have the family waiting in a private room. Prepare the body in case the family wants to see him now."

Dread filled Elizabeth when she learned the doctor had requested a private meeting. "He's going to tell us that Ted is dead."

"But we have to talk to him," Frank gently urged his reluctant wife.

"Maybe he's going to tell us about the brain surgery," she answered.

That's it, she thought, grabbing onto any frail hope. *He's going to tell us what they need to do. He's just going to talk about that.*

To an observer, Elizabeth looked as cool as ice as she walked to the waiting room. Inside, volcanic emotions pressured a frayed psyche, finding release in a pitiful wail that escaped her lips when Dr. Bond walked in and shook his head.

"Ted didn't make it. His injuries were too severe," Dr. Bond said softly. "His heart couldn't handle it. He died at 2:20."

Frank could not help looking at his watch. It was 2:30. *He's only been gone ten minutes—I didn't even know it—and it already seems a lifetime.*

Elizabeth rocked in her chair, weeping and hitting the back of her head against the concrete wall. She remembered Ted as a baby, nestled against her breast; the day her Cub Scout son came into the kitchen clutching a withered bouquet of flowers; the night he was baptized by his father. There was absolutely no solace to be found except in the knowledge that although her son may be dead to this life, he was still alive in eternity. As of a few minutes ago, he waited for her. *And I can go to him.* Then raw emotions overwhelmed her again.

Frank's grief gave way to concern for Elizabeth. "Can you give her anything?" he asked the doctor, fearful that she might harm herself.

"No. It's better if she gets through this without a sedative," Dr. Bond said.

Through her emotional haze, Elizabeth heard the doctor tell them that Ted's body had been cleaned for immediate viewing. Both declined the offer to view their son's body in the emergency room. Later Frank and Elizabeth would regret this decision. *I don't think I can stand any of this,* Elizabeth thought as she shook her head back and forth, muttering, "No . . . , no . . . , no."

Frank asked Tim to bring Ted's body home.

"What funeral home?"

The question shook Frank to the core. *Funeral home?* It would be the first of many decisions he would be forced to make concerning his son's death. There had never been a thought of a funeral home; maybe a fleeting concern about where he and Elizabeth would be buried. But Ted? Everything had happened so quickly that this moment of decision took on an air of unreality.

"That's something that never enters your mind: your son's death," he said. "What funeral home? Henninger's, I guess."

Conversation between the Morrises and the Hunters on the ride home was sporadic. Frank and Elizabeth were slowly coming to grips with their son's death. A funeral had to be planned.

"Always remember that Ted was a Christian young man," Plomer Hunter gently said. "In God's eyes it's not the length of life, but the quality."

All of them recalled the last moments they shared with the young man.

"I saw him at the mall this morning—yesterday morning," Ruth Hunter said. "He was taking a break, drinking a soda. I teased him about staying out late, because he looked sleepy."

Elizabeth's eyes lit up with a new horror. "We've got to tell my father!"

Ted had been named for both his grandfathers—Theodore Alverson and Roy Joseph Martin Morris. His job at the Sound Shop had brought him close to his maternal grandparents, since he ate Sunday dinner with them after church. Many Saturdays found him mowing their lawn. His Grandfather Alverson, seventy-five, was in ill health after having suffered a heart attack.

"Frank," she said, vocalizing her fears. "This could upset him so much that he might have another heart attack . . . and die."

He did collapse in the bathroom, in spite of their best efforts to break the news gently. Elizabeth found her father doubled over the commode. Her already overburdened system demanded that she run screaming out of the room, but she held her frayed emotions in check.

I could lose both of them, she thought as she struggled to help him rise. *Not him, too!* her mind screamed.

Medication calmed the distraught grandfather's racing heart. Soon he returned to as near normal as his grief would allow.

When Plomer Hunter let the Morrises out by their automobile in the hospital parking lot, the pair had just finished a whispered huddle.

"It would please us, and I think it would please Ted, too, if you would conduct the funeral service," Frank said.

Plomer looked at the depth of pain in Frank's eyes. He had had to perform many difficult tasks in the past, but this was going to be one of the hardest. It would be difficult not only because Ted had died—he knew the young man's Christian life-style—but because of his love for Frank and Elizabeth. Would they ever be able to accept the scriptural truth of Psalms 116:15: "Precious in the sight of the Lord is the death of his saints"?

Plomer and Frank had virtually grown up together. At twenty, Plomer took his first full-time preaching job at Little River Church of Christ. When Plomer moved to another con-. gregation, the families remained in touch, often seeing each other at various church-related events. Frank married and moved into the country. He, Elizabeth, and Ted began worshiping at Cadiz a few years after Plomer became the minister there. Plomer returned to Little River in 1981 and eventually convinced Frank and Elizabeth to join him there. The small congregation had special needs, one of them being a song leader. It was an offer Frank could not refuse, so the family started making the twenty-five-mile drive to Little River. *If there is one thing that can sustain this couple, it is the biblical certainty that they can go to their son.*

"It will be a privilege," Plomer said softly. "I won't let you down."

"We know that," Frank said.

"And thank you for tonight," Elizabeth added, reaching out to pat Ruth's shoulder. "I don't know how we would have made it without you."

An unspoken communication concerning Ruth's dream passed

between the two women. It would be many weeks before they could freely discuss it.

Then the Morrises got into their car. They both knew that they had just taken the first steps of a long, lonely journey. Had anyone told them the strange twists their lives would follow the next few years, they would not have believed it, nor would they have cared. For them, there was only one reality: They knew that their son would never again go home with them.

What a sad, sad morning. Plomer wiped away the tears as he watched their automobile disappear out of sight. Ruth was silent as they drove home. When he pulled into the driveway, she turned to her husband.

"That dream. . . ." She did not have to finish.

The house was still lit with a cheery Christmas glow when the Morrises pulled into the driveway. The multicolored brilliance of the lights suddenly seemed obscene, so Frank unplugged them. The two grimly sat down in the living room. What was there to say? What was there to do?

Elizabeth idly studied the joyous Christmas decorations she'd so lovingly placed around the living room. *But there is no joy in this home.* Her mind's eye could see Ted bounding down the stairs, then hustling back up to straighten a bit of garland. She could still feel his presence as he teased her while rattling Christmas presents less than twenty-four hours before. Everywhere she looked, she saw Ted.

Suddenly she jumped to her feet, rushed across the living room, and started wildly tearing the garland off the stairway.

"Eliza—" Stunned at first, Frank immediately realized what she was doing. He watched until her arms were loaded with garland and she turned to him.

"Go into the kitchen and get some paper bags. We're taking

this down,'' she exclaimed, a hysterical edge to her voice. ''This is not a house of joy.''

After they had cleared the house of decorations, with the exception of the Christmas tree and its gifts, they dropped into bed, exhausted. But sleep was slow to come. After long minutes, Frank felt Elizabeth get up. He heard her go upstairs and into Ted's bedroom. She was gone so long that. Frank was trying to decide if he should check on her when he heard her returning. Quietly, she lay down as he elected not to intrude upon her solitude.

In the darkness he could not see that she had brought back one of Ted's ties, a red one that he wore often. She clasped it to her face, breathing deeply of its lingering aroma, until finally, with the scent of her son fresh in her nostrils, she fell into a fitful sleep.

Larry Webb's father awakened him at 6:00 A.M. on December 24.

Something's wrong! Larry could tell by the look on his father's face.

''Ted . . . .'' Earl Webb could not go on. Finally he explained, ''He's dead.''

A flood of adrenaline pounded Larry so hard that he could not be still. He jumped out of bed and ran into another room; his father could hear him weeping. What Earl Webb did not fully comprehend was the clash of emotions battering his young son. Only later would he learn that Larry had almost spent the night with Ted. Did the decision not to spend the night cost Ted his life, because the young men would have gone by Larry's house first? Or would Larry also have died in the crash? Or was it sheer chance that Larry went a different route that night and was not right in front of or behind Ted?

In the lonely hours of mourning, Larry even considered the consequences of the way each of them had parked his automobile at the downtown restaurant. Did an action as capricious as the direction a driver parked his car mean death for one and life for the other?

In their profound grief, the Morrises had failed to inform most of Frank's family, so Frank's sister, Gladys Rose, living in nearby Clarksville, learned of the death of her nephew on the radio.

Elizabeth heard the same radio broadcast as she made coffee after their restless night. They sipped the hot liquid for a few moments before Elizabeth reached into her robe pocket and pulled out a clipping.

"I found this last night when I went into Ted's room. I couldn't believe it was there. It was lying on his desk. He must have just clipped it out and put it there," she explained, tentatively shoving the clip in front of Frank. "It was eerie to read it."

It was an Ann Landers column devoted to the death of a teenager in an automobile accident. Written in the first person, "Dead at Seventeen" is a poignant tale of tragedy.

Frank realized that his son was not the hapless youth portrayed in the column, but the similarities between the two teenage deaths shook him. *I can't believe she discovered this on his desk only hours after he died.* Shaking the thought aside, he suggested, "Let's go to the police station and see what we can find out."

Tommy awoke with a cotton mouth. *I need a drink,* he thought. But it was water he wanted, not liquor. This was the first time in years that alcohol did not appeal to him.

Besides, I need a clear head; no telling what's going to happen next.

His head throbbed from the stitches in his scalp. His body felt as if someone had beaten him with a sledgehammer: every bone felt bruised, every muscle ached as he limped into the kitchen.

He heard his stepfather answer the telephone, but he could not understand the muffled conversation. Phelps met him in the hallway. "I think you'd better come in here," Phelps said, indicating their bedroom. Tommy found his mother seated on the side of the bed, gently crying.

"Ted Morris is dead, and the police have charged you with murder," Phelps said, with an acerbic tinge in his voice. "That was the sheriff's office. They're ready to come pick you up, or we can bring you down."

Tommy's fear was like a physical blow, so strong that he gasped for breath. Dumbfounded, he stood staring at them. *What am I going to do?* Finally he fell to his knees, great heaving sobs racking his body. Tommy crawled the few feet to his mother, putting his head in her lap.

"This is something you're going to have to live with your whole life." Judy sighed, carefully stroking his bandaged head. Immediately she wished she had not said that, but she was so full of hatred at what Tommy's drinking had done that she wanted him to realize the serious consequences of his actions.

"I wish it had been me instead of him," Tommy said between moaning sobs.

It really would have been better if it had been. Stunned that she could even think such a thought, Judy fell silent.

He was a criminal who had been caught, and Tommy's remorse centered on retribution. He feared the justice system and the possibility of spending the rest of his life in jail.

If only I had stayed home. If only they had kept my car keys.
His soul ached from the desire to change his actions of the previous night. But the one thing he did not wish was that he had not
had a drink that night, and right then, as he wept at his mother's
knee, Tommy Pigage wanted a drink.

Miles away, Elizabeth Morris dressed to go to the police station. She went to her jewelry box, where she fished out a long
gold chain. She slipped Ted's high school senior ring from her
finger, threaded the chain through it, and hooked the necklace
around her neck.

Judy drove Tommy directly to the police station, where he was
rushed into booking.
A police officer patted him down, his hands probing Tommy's
body for hidden weapons.
"Put your things in this," another officer commanded, thrust-
ing a cloth bag into Tommy's hands.
*They have no feelings for anyone. To them everyone's a crim-
inal.*
Mug shots. Front! Left profile! Right profile! The commands
were rough, no-nonsense, and demanded immediate compliance.
They're making me feel just like a criminal.
Fingerprints! The officer called off each digit as he stained the
fingerpad, then rolled it onto the fingerprint card, leaving an inky
map of the surface of each digit.
This is what they do to criminals!
Tommy looked at the officer gripping his hand.
*He thinks I'm some kind of lowlife! He's treating me like
dirt.*
With a growing sense of doom, Tommy realized that each

step of the booking process brought him closer to his worst nightmare: jail. He had no doubt that his life would be a living horror when he landed in a jail cell. Gentle by nature, Tommy knew he did not have the street smarts to survive life with desperate men.

He had heard of homosexual rape, of forced sodomy, even of murder, and in jail he feared that there might be a fate worse than death, once he was put among these primitive people. *My days are numbered. I'll be killed in prison. Why me?* he wailed inside. *What have I done to deserve all this?*

Fresh from reconstructing the automobile crash at the death scene, Officer Bob Breathitt took Tommy to a holding area in a stairwell just outside the cells. It had a desk, table, and chairs. The officer was repelled by the lingering smell of alcohol that permeated Tommy's presence.

Breathitt took Tommy's history, curt but polite. He had no inclination for small talk. "Wait here. The bondsman will be here shortly," he said upon completing the report.

Finally alone, Tommy did find some relief in the fact that he had not been put in a cell. He was still behind bars, but it was not a cell he had to share with criminals.

The stress of the past few hours and the lack of sleep began to take their toll. Tommy rested his head on his arms on the table. His mind rambled.

Why me? I'm just a "regular Joe." I've never bothered anyone. I'm not a criminal. I don't hate anyone. I didn't want anything bad to happen.

As he had since the deadly crash, he reasoned that he was really blameless. *It was just an accident. I didn't do anything on purpose. It was just an accident. Why is everyone so upset over an accident? Sure, the boy died. I'm sorry he died. But it was just an accident.*

Next he blamed some unknown fate that seemed to plague his life. *It was just terrible luck. Why do I always have to have terrible luck? Why couldn't I have made it home? Why do these things always happen to me? Why can't people just leave me alone?*

Restless, the Morrises went to the Hopkinsville police station to learn more about the accident. The receptionist's daughter had known Ted, so they waited only a few seconds before they found themselves seated across the desk from Chief of Police Frank Boyer.

"I'm sorry at your loss," the chief said, waiting for them to set the tone of the conversation.

"I want you to know that Ted was a good boy," Elizabeth began earnestly.

"You don't have to tell me that. Several officers have already been by to tell me that they knew your son and that he was a fine person," the chief reassured them.

What a nice, caring man, Elizabeth thought.

"We want to know more about the accident," Frank began.

"We've had men on the scene since first light," Boyer assured the Morrises. "Everyone was contacted when we learned that Ted had died. Murder charges have already been filed."

"Murder?" Frank was surprised, but pleased.

"You don't know?"

"We don't know anything."

"Except that our son is dead," Elizabeth interjected.

As gently as he could, the chief explained. "Your son was killed by a drunken driver."

"Drunk?" The word burned in the pit of Frank's stomach.

"There's no doubt that he was drunk. We just have to determine how drunk, and a technician took a blood sample at the hospital. It has already been sent to Atlanta for testing; not only for alcohol, but for drugs as well,'' Boyer said.

The Morrises said nothing. Their silence made the police chief uncomfortable. It is never an easy job to tell grieving parents how their child died, so he might as well tell them the rest of it. ''The man driving the other vehicle was Tommy Pigage. He came through it with just a gash on his forehead,'' he added, hesitating a second to let them assimilate that information.

''Apparently he passed out. The investigating officer says Pigage claims that he doesn't remember a thing,'' he continued. ''He was driving on the wrong side of the street when he hit your son head-on.''

That means it really wasn't an accident, Frank concluded. *This is something that could have been avoided. All that Pig . . . , Piggy . . . ,* his mind stumbled over the unfamiliar name. *All he had to do was not drink. It was no accident. The chief's right. It was murder.*

''Can we have a copy of the report?'' Frank wanted to see for himself.

''Sure.'' The chief asked his secretary to make a copy and continued to explain that the jaws of life were used to free Ted and that the accident happened on Canton Pike.

''We drove right by where it happened,'' Elizabeth said with a small gasp. ''But we didn't see anything.''

''They clean those things up fast,'' the chief said.

''This guy who killed Ted. How old is he?'' Frank asked.

''Twenty-four.''

''He's already lived six years longer than my Ted,'' Elizabeth said to no one in particular.

"I've never heard of murder charges for driving under the influence." Frank was astonished and delighted, but he remained a bit confused over what he considered unusual charges.

"I believe it's justified in this case. Besides, we've had three officers investigate and study the law. This was their recommendation," Boyer explained.

"Is he in jail? I don't want him to hurt anyone else," Elizabeth said.

"He is being processed as we speak."

"Will they put him in jail?"

"I don't know, Mrs. Morris. It's likely that he will be released on bond."

"You mean he has killed my son and he won't spend one night in jail?"

"That's up to the judge at his bail hearing."

"At least you're trying to mete out justice," Frank said, getting up to leave. "We thank you and your men."

They were still assimilating the information as they walked to the car. Elizabeth had been strangely quiet. Frank opened the door for her, but before she got in, she turned to her husband and blurted, "I hope they give him the electric chair."

"At least the law is on our side. Maybe they'll put him away so he won't hurt anyone else," Frank answered.

"I'd pull the switch, if they'd let me." There was a macabre finality in that statement that startled Frank. He had never seen this side of his wife. For twenty years he had experienced the compassionate, tender Elizabeth, the young girl he had fallen in love with the first time he had seen her, disheveled and helping a girlfriend deliver newspapers. Her statement disturbed him.

"The law will handle it for us," he reassured her.

"I hope so."

The couple decided to drop off a picture of Ted at the local newspaper office. Frank discovered a Christmas party in progress. It was an acute reminder of the juxtaposition of their tragedy to Christmas felicity.

After five hours in jail, Tommy was officially charged with murder. A $10,000 bond was set. He was released on his own recognizance, a ruling that meant he did not have to pay even 10 percent of the bond. He was ordered to appear in court three days later, December 27, 1982.

When Tommy Pigage walked out of jail, he was a man with a mission. He did not call his family or a friend. He knew where he wanted to be and what he needed, so he walked briskly through the town toward his apartment, which was less than a mile away.

For the first time, he imagined the eyes of hostile people, fierce, uncompromising eyes. It seemed to him that peering eyes scrutinized his every step. He believed that everyone in town knew what had happened and that they hated him for it. It was a long walk, and although the weather was chilly, he began to feel sweat oozing out his pores. The salty perspiration stung the neatly sutured cuts in his head. His body still ached from the blows it had sustained as he lay unconscious during the wreck. He was fearful that he might black out now, but he stubbornly put one foot in front of another, concentrating on reaching his apartment. When it came into view, his pace became brisker. He was able to maintain control as he walked up the stairs. Quivering hands fumbled with the key before he opened the door and slipped into the darkened safety of the apartment, shutting out the rest of the world.

Where is it? He found it by the bed, where he had left it less than twenty-four hours ago on his dresser. With a sigh of relief, Tommy Pigage did not even take the time to use a glass or dash the liquid over ice; he took a long, appreciative pull of lukewarm bourbon right out of the bottle. *I need this,* he thought. *I feel terrible.*

But it did not keep him from feeling like a caged animal. There was no escape. His mind tried to comprehend the unknown paths of the future. It was no use trying. If he did not know what was going to happen the next day, how could he comprehend anything past that? There was a temporary escape, and he used it. He took another long pull from the bottle he had purchased the day before. Soon he was submerged in the artificial glow of alcohol and its mind-numbing release.

Why don't people just leave me alone?

Dale and Lou Ann Rogers were headed out of town when they heard the news of Ted's death on the radio. They immediately drove to the Morrises, where they found Elizabeth trying to muster enough courage to go into Ted's room and select suitable clothing to take to the funeral home.

"I just don't think I can do it," she told Lou Ann.

"I'll go with you," her dear friend said.

Lou Ann watched as Elizabeth selected a pinstripe suit Ted's grandmother had purchased for his high school graduation; shirt, underclothes, and socks completed the ensemble.

Ruth Hunter and her son, Jimmy, joined the mourning parents at the funeral home as Frank and Elizabeth selected a metallic blue casket later that morning.

Jerry Morgan, minister at the Southside Church of Christ, would be asked to assist Plomer Hunter in the service. Frank wanted "Leaning on the Everlasting Arms" in the song service, and Elizabeth selected "Farther Along" and "Be With Me, Lord."

It was decided to have the service in the funeral home chapel, which could seat 250 people.

"Have . . . ?" Elizabeth did not know how to ask this question. "Is . . . ?" Again a long pause. Finally she blurted it out, "Have you seen Ted?"

"Yes."

"Can we have the casket open?"

"Yes, but we will have to use makeup on his left cheek," Henninger explained. "You can touch his hands. It will be all right as long as no one touches his face."

Elizabeth looked quizzical.

"We will have to use putty and makeup," he said gently.

The Morrises nodded their understanding.

"When will he be ready?" Frank asked.

"Tomorrow. About four. I suggest that the family come at three so you can have an hour of private time."

Everyone silently noted that it would be Christmas Day.

Before Ruth and Jimmy Hunter left, they gave the Morrises a sack containing additional items from Ted's car, along with a toolbox they had found in the trunk. The sack contained an umbrella and several cassette tapes. Now that Ted was gone, Elizabeth could not bear to part with anything that was Ted's, even tiny scraps of paper found in his automobile. There would be several other expeditions to the smashed vehicle, including a personal search by the grieving mother, before Elizabeth would be satisfied.

Christmas Eve was a joyous day turned bitter for Judy Anderson.

"I keep thinking about the Morrises," she told Phelps. "They don't have their son, and I know they have a tree, and I know they have Christmas presents, and I know they won't even be opened."

"It's a mess," Phelps acknowledged the sense of gloom that had settled over the household. The family had begun to view Tommy as a hopeless case. "He's destroying his life."

"If I had been a better mother, maybe he would not be having this problem," she retorted.

With the exception of a few concerned remarks from his brothers, the subject of the accident was taboo when Tommy was picked up that night. The family did not know how to handle Tommy, so an unspoken conspiracy was forged to neglect the incident. What else could be done? Tommy had been forced to leave home because of his drinking; his contact with family members was at a minimum because of his drinking; and now his drinking had finally killed someone.

It was a strained evening. After dinner Tommy escaped to the front porch, where he nursed a beer. Judy had been trying to find time alone with him without being too obvious. She pulled up a chair and looked across the massive front yard, softly aglow with colored lights. She could barely make out the rows of regal maple trees that flanked each side of the long drive leading to the house.

Tommy really looked forward to moving here and having a family, she mused, then laughed out loud.

"What's so funny?" he asked.

"Do you remember when we first moved here?"

"Sure."

"Do you remember that you thought Phelps and I should have a baby?"

"Maybe you should have," he had to grin at the thought, but she noticed a change in his voice.

Was there a tinge of regret, of bitterness? she wondered.

"You played baseball and football, and you ran around with your brothers," she continued to reminisce. "You were always such a sweet boy, such a kind disposition. I know that we had some troubled times . . . ."

Judy's voice trailed off.

But something happened to Tommy. Maybe he believed Phelps failed him. Maybe he believed I failed him. Maybe I was too busy working to devote time to him. Something happened that turned that sweet young boy with high expectations into. . . . Into what? And why?

Tommy turned to look at his mother, a petite woman with a quick smile that flashed a dimple in her left cheek, short-cropped blond hair—now lost in thought.

I believe she always wanted to be a good mother.

"What happened?" she asked when he caught her eye. "Tommy, what happened?"

He considered the question, his mind roaming across the years, then sighed. "I don't know."

They sat in silence, each consumed by the search for an answer, although each instinctively knew it would take a greater frankness than each was willing to invest at that moment to forge an honest answer.

"It's chilly. Maybe we'd better go back in," Tommy said. This was not a discussion he relished.

"There's something I have to ask you. No, I want to suggest that you do it," she said, carefully picking her words. She knew his temper, and in this rare moment of sharing she did not want to kindle it. "Are you going to talk to the parents of the boy you killed?"

"What?" *That's the last thing I want to do.*

"I think you should," she said.

"I wouldn't know what to say."

" 'I'm sorry' would be a good start."

"If someone had killed me, would you want to talk to them?"

"I don't know. Maybe."

There is no way I'm going to do this. I'd run away if I thought it would do any good. The farther I am away from those people, the better I like it.

"Well?"

Humor her! "Sure, if you think it's best," he lied, noticing the relief in her face. *Somehow she wants her family to be absolved of this or at least to do the right thing.*

When they went inside, Tommy found another beer. The thought of dealing with the Morrises was both physically and emotionally terrifying.

That night, longtime friend Joe Dunn made a special trip to see Frank and Elizabeth. He had sensed the mood of the town. He had a suggestion when he finally got Frank to one side. "Don't hold services at the funeral chapel," he said. "It just will not be large enough to hold the crowd."

Instead, he suggested the 650-seat Southside Church of Christ building. "And even that may not be large enough," he warned. Puzzled, Frank agreed to the change; he had given no thought to how many people might attend Ted's funeral.

Friends and families had visited the Morrises throughout the day, arriving hourly with sympathy cards, potted plants, food, and a desire to ease, if not share, the family's grief. Each friend brought a new wave of mourning, so by the end of the day, the Morrises were exhausted. They were in no mood to attend any Christmas Eve gathering. They knew their presence would be a damper on any celebration, so they elected to remain home alone.

A numbing—almost physical—depression had settled over the pair. Perhaps it was a mild state of shock. In less than twenty-four hours they had suffered the death of a son, had had only snatches of sleep, learned that their son was killed by a drunken driver, and handled funeral arrangements.

Once alone, Elizabeth hugged Frank, her head on his shoulder. "Pray, Frank," she said. "Pray aloud."

And he did, fervently asking for strength, but mostly for understanding. He concluded: "We know that You have promised not to tempt or test us beyond what we are able to endure. We just don't know how we can endure any more. We know that all things work together for those who love the Lord. I don't understand that, but we pray with all our hearts that we will come to find the good." His voice choked as tears began to well up in his eyes. He clenched them tightly to overcome the emotion and continued the prayer as little rivulets eased down his cheek and into Elizabeth's hair. "One thing I do know is that we have a new understanding of what You suffered at the death of Your Son. Since You are our Creator and Supreme Ruler of all that exists, and the Holy One, how much greater would have been Your anguish, than ours. We know that Ted is with You. We will do everything we can to come to him. We pray these things in the name of Your Son, Jesus Christ, our Savior. Amen."

There was comfort in knowing that a caring Creator's heart wept with them. Frank could feel Elizabeth gently sobbing. It was not the tumultuous mourning that occurs at the onset of death, it was almost a tranquil release. Afraid to break the moment, he held her gently as their tears mingled.

Finally she looked into his face. "We're exhausted."

He nodded agreement. As he led her to the bedroom, she picked up the sack Ruth and Jimmy Hunter had given them at the funeral home. In their room, she dumped the sack, its contents sprawling across the bed.

The action bothered Frank. A meticulous accounting of the bag's contents would have been more in Elizabeth's nature. He could see she was already immersed in checking out each item, yet only a few moments before she had said she was exhausted and ready to go to bed. She was not behaving in character.

Don't be so trivial at a time like this, he scolded himself. *Everyone handles grief differently.* He dressed for bed with the idea of giving her a few minutes alone with the contents of the paper grocery sack.

"Frank." She said his name softly. He turned to see her holding a cassette tape in her hand. "Here," she held out the tape.

Puzzled, he took it. His hand felt the cellophane still wrapped around it. *It's unopened.* And with that thought, came the realization that he was holding his Christmas gift from Ted. It was a T. G. Shepherd tape, just as he had hinted. *He probably put it in his car last night. He probably was going to wrap it Christmas morning.* "It's . . . ," Frank started.

"I know," Elizabeth said tenderly, before adding in a whisper, "I know."

Her heart ached. Their lives had become an emotional roller

coaster. Just when it appeared that their sorrow was under control, new anguish engulfed them.

"One last gift." Frank wondered if he would ever be able to listen to the country singer's music without deep remorse.

"I wish he had had the chance to buy my cookbook," she said.

"But he did."

"He did?" Elizabeth was surprised. "Where is it?"

"I don't know. He told me yesterday that he had bought the cookbook."

"It's not here." Elizabeth swept her arm to indicate the items on the bed.

"Maybe they found it and put it away," Frank suggested.

"I don't think so. Jimmy searched last night. He and Ruth searched this morning. They didn't find it," she explained, a thought chilling her. "Do you think someone who moved the car might have taken it? Or someone who was on the scene of the accident?"

"I don't think so. Why take a cookbook?"

The thought that someone might steal from a death car was degrading, a disgrace to humanity. But it could have happened.

"If it's not in the car, then it's here, in this house," she said, springing into action, rejuvenated at the thought. "It has to be in his room. Frank, I have to have it. It was the last thing he ever bought me," she said. "And I want it right now!"

They went upstairs to begin a systematic search of Ted's room.

"Be careful, Frank. Don't disturb anything too much," she instructed. "I want everything left just like it was the day he walked out of here."

The minutes turned to hours, because they were careful not to disturb anything.

Saturday
December 25, 1982

Midnight passed, but still no cookbook.

"Frank, look," Elizabeth commanded, pointing toward Ted's desk.

When he looked, he realized Elizabeth was not pointing at the desk, but at the clock. Its digital face showed 2:20. It had been twenty-four hours—one day without Ted. The first day of the rest of their lives had just passed.

The couple decided that maybe Ted had left the cookbook at the mall. They would check the next morning. They abandoned the search, not able to bear being in Ted's room at this exact moment.

And for the second night, sleep would only come in bits and snatches.

On Christmas morning gifts were opened with appropriate appreciation, but Christmas dinner was a farce. Judy Anderson watched as her family fled after a day of forced gaiety.

Tommy sought the artificial happiness of his easy chair, his television, and a fresh bottle of bourbon.

Although he did not want to know what was being reported by the news media, even an alcoholic haze could not dull his curiosity. He had read the *Kentucky New Era* newspaper account of the accident, and it had angered him. The story said that Tommy had been charged with murder, that the crash had occurred on the wrong side of the road, that Tommy remembered nothing, and that a blood sample had been taken to determine if Tommy had been drinking.

Why are they out to get me? he wondered in a paranoia born of drink and nurtured by an alcoholic's desire for justification. It was Tommy against an uncaring, uncompromising world that would never give him a chance to simply find peace his own way. *They don't care about me. They don't care about how I feel about it.*

He had received no telephone calls from reporters, but he knew he would not have submitted to an interview if someone had called. Also, he conveniently forgot, as he wallowed in self-pity, that he had put his telephone under a mound of pillows. He could not be contacted, because he did not want to be disturbed.

If I were a reporter, I'd sure do a better job than what they've done, he justified his anger.

Although 3:00 P.M. was designated family time, Frank and Elizabeth decided to arrive several hours early, to be alone with their son. They anticipated that only a few friends would give up a portion of Christmas Day to come to the funeral home at 4:00 P.M. for the visitation hour. Devoutly religious, the Morrises understood that Ted's body no longer harbored his soul, that his body was now an earthly shell that would return to nature. But his body was all that they had ever known of him on this earth, and they were determined to spend a last few minutes alone with the only vestige they had ever known of their son.

The parents mourned anew at the sight of Ted in a casket. The juxtaposition of their young son in a house of death seemed almost incomprehensible. Death belonged to the aged, not the young.

"Frank, where is Ted right now? At this very instant, as we speak. Where do you think he is?" Elizabeth asked.

Before he could say anything, Elizabeth added another question that would haunt her: "Will Ted know me when I join him? Will he know me as his mother?" An even more dreadful thought: "Will I know Ted? I want to know Ted in heaven."

"The Bible. . . ."

"Frank," Elizabeth was not even looking at him. Her eyes were fixed on her dead son. "Why did God do this? What did I do to make God do this to me? Several ladies have told me that this is God's will." Her voice raised perceptibly, quivering. "That Ted's death is God's will! Frank, why would God kill an eighteen-year-old boy?"

There was a long silence. Frank wanted to make sure she was finished. "Elizabeth," he started as she turned her eyes to his, "the Lord says we will never be tempted beyond what we can bear. I have to be honest: I feel right now like I've gone beyond that. But I do know two things."

Elizabeth waited.

"I know that the answers to all your questions are in the Bible, and we will study to find those answers. I suspect I already know some of them, but right here, right now, is not the time to discuss it in depth. We'll wait until we're home. We'll open our Bibles, and we will study.

"The second thing I know—and Elizabeth, I know this with all my heart—is that God doesn't kill eighteen-year-old boys. Satan does. It was not God that killed Ted. It was the work of Satan that killed Ted, and I know that as sure as we are standing here."

She rushed into his arms with a whispered, "Pray, Frank.

Just pray." They stood there, praying quietly, until an attendant notified them that several friends had arrived to pay their respects.

Frank and Elizabeth were stunned when the doors opened to reveal a number of friends who had come more than two hours before the start of public mourning. For the next seven hours, the grieving parents would be consoled by a continuous line of friends, at times stretching out the funeral home door. Some friends patiently waited more than four hours for a chance to express their condolences.

I can't believe so many people would give up their Christmas Day to come here. Elizabeth found great comfort in this amazing outpouring of sympathy.

It was beneficial, yet a physical and emotional drain for the parents. For more than two days they had had little sleep. Now they stood, shaking hands, taking a few moments to visit with each well-wisher. Finally, after several days of mourning, their bodies started to reach exhaustion.

"Remember Ted," she told one friend. It was a theme that would come to consume Elizabeth.

"Don't forget Ted," she said over and over as each friend passed by.

One elderly friend hugged Elizabeth.

"God called him home," she told her. "It was God's will."

She started to reply, and Frank reached over to take Elizabeth's hand to give it a gentle squeeze. She found strength in Frank's understanding and squashed her retort. *Frank is right, it was Satan's will.*

The pair found special comfort in the young people who came to pay their respects. All had known Ted, and all had a special memory of Ted to share with the Morrises. Frank found himself concentrating on the relationship between each mourner and his son. Each sad face brought a new wave of anguish, and Frank came to realize that he and Elizabeth were trapped in an emotional whirlwind. *You can hardly let one wave of grief pass until another one overcomes you,* he thought.

Although physically exhausting, the Morrises also found the long day to be spiritually renewing. They found themselves surrounded by an emotional cocoon of love, as each mourner bound another fiber of healing compassion around their broken hearts.

Tommy Pigage continued to brood, but on this day he could find no escape. The *Kentucky New Era* ran an obituary. A picture from a happier time showed a smiling Ted Morris in tuxedo and ruffled shirt. It was the first time Tommy had had a chance to study the image of the young man he had killed.

Also, his mother had loosed a new demon in his life. He had lied to her about contacting the family, but now he could not shake the growing need to apologize to Ted's parents. Common sense born of drink, however, told him that there was nothing he could do.

How can I approach them?

Telephone. What do I say? How do I keep them from hanging up on me?

A letter. No matter what I wrote it would not be good enough.

I could see them in person, just drive out in the country to their house and knock on the door. How would they react? I'd probably get a fist in the face, if not worse.

There's really no good way. It's hopeless.

By the end of the day, Tommy had decided that the less he knew about the Morrises, the safer he would be. It would be better to hide and not deal with the situation. He also justified his decision by convincing himself that any approach to the Morrises would be hopeless. *The best thing to do is to leave them alone, and maybe they'll leave me alone,* he concluded as he drank himself into a stupor.

Sunday
December 26, 1982

"And we know that all things work together for good to them that love God, to them who are the called according to his purpose."

Challenged to help his grieving congregation, Plomer Hunter chose Romans 8:28 as the sermon text the day of the funeral.

"While all things work together for good, we need to remember that not all things are good," Plomer began. "But if we love the Lord, even tragedy can work out for good." He went on to explore the reciprocal relationship with God that sustains an anguished believer in times of emotional stress.

While Frank found great comfort in the sermon, Elizabeth was unable to keep her mind on it. She glanced over at Ruth, remembering her tears a week ago over her dream of Ted's death. She chided herself because she had no foreboding of her son's death, no last farewell, except in a fading memory. Now she realized that in a few hours her son would disappear from sight. *All I'll have then are photographs and memories,* she reflected. *But you can be with him again. And you can be with him again because of what happened 2,000 years ago in Jer-*

usalem and what happened in the Cadiz church building seven years ago.

She picked up her Bible and leafed through it, to John 3:16.

"For God so loved the world, that he gave his only begotten Son, that whosoever believeth in him should not perish, but have everlasting life."

Elizabeth knew it was a much-quoted Scripture taken from the context of Christ's secret meeting with Nicodemus, a religious ruler of the Jews. Like so many of his fellow countrymen, he had not understood that Christ came to establish a spiritual kingdom through which He would rule the world.

God's son was killed 2,000 years ago as a human sacrifice, the ultimate offering for mankind's sin, she reasoned. Everyone who elects to benefit from that godly sacrifice has eternal salvation.

As does Ted. Her mind drifted back seven years, to the night an eleven-year-old Ted slipped his dad a note as a Wednesday evening service came to a close in Cadiz.

"Please baptize me, but all the people I want in there is me and you," the note had read. Frank took Elizabeth's hand in his, and when she drew it back, she found the note. After services, Ted consented to have Plomer and Ruth Hunter and a few of his young friends remain for the baptism.

Elizabeth was joined in the front row by the small group of well-wishers. Frank and Ted dressed in white coveralls the congregation kept for baptisms.

"Ted, do you believe that Jesus Christ is the Son of God?"

"Yes, sir, I do."

"Based on that confession and your desire to obey God's law, I now baptize you in the name of the Father, and the Son, and the Holy Ghost for the remission of your sins."

Frank cupped his hand over Ted's mouth and pinched his nostrils together as he lowered his son under the water. Elizabeth softly cried tears of joy.

"Amen," Frank said as he raised Ted out of the water.

"Amen," echoed Ted's adolescent voice.

"Amen," Elizabeth added softly.

Ted had hugged his dad. It was a solemn moment, but Frank had grinned as he looked across the top of his son's head and into his wife's eyes. The proud parents knew that their son had made the most important decision he would ever make in his lifetime. It was a scene that Elizabeth cherished; father and son hugging. It was a peaceful moment to which she often escaped, because it held within it eternal hope.

Elizabeth was so deep in thought that Frank had to gently poke her to stand for the invitation song at the close of Plomer's sermon.

She took his hand, still staring at the baptistery.

Will I ever be able to see the familiar without seeing Ted?

Frank and Elizabeth were immediately surrounded by fellow Christians when services ended. It was the first time many members of the Little River Church of Christ had had a chance to offer condolences.

"It's God's will," a well-meaning sister patted Elizabeth's hand. The well-intentioned phrase shot through her like an electric jolt. *Why would God want my son? Ted was a good son. Why would God take him? Why would it be God's will that my son die because someone got drunk and drove a car when he shouldn't have?* For a fleeting moment she almost snapped out her thoughts, but in that split second of tumultuous emotions, another stunned her: *Maybe God is punishing me!*

Frank looked on in concern. It was taking Elizabeth too long to answer.

Finally Elizabeth returned the pat. "Thank you," was her only reply.

As soon as they could free themselves, the Morrises went to the Alverson home to grab a bite to eat. They circled by Frank's parents for a brief time, then went to the Southside Church of Christ.

"We want to get back to where Ted is," Frank told his understanding family.

Anticipating a few moments alone with their son's body, the grieving parents were surprised to discover the church sanctuary rapidly filling with mourners. More than one hundred floral tributes surrounded the casket and spilled into the aisles. The couple was immediately surrounded by friends offering comfort. Within a matter of minutes, a line extended the length of the sanctuary as friends filed by the couple and then the casket.

"Don't forget Ted," Elizabeth heard herself repeat the message of the night before. It was all she could say. "Don't forget Ted."

Mourners were standing in the aisles and overflowed into the back foyer of the packed church building, delaying the scheduled start. Southside minister Jerry Morgan realized that the couple could not take their seats without offending well-wishers, so he gently approached Frank and Elizabeth.

"Could you take your seats?" he urged, giving the couple an excuse to rejoin their family. "We can't get started until all Ted's friends have paid their last respects."

If only I could have told you "I love you" one more time, Elizabeth thought, laying her hand on Ted's chest in one last farewell.

The grateful Morrises fled to the family section. As a gospel quartet began to sing, the sound of pounding rain drifted into the building.

Tearful angels. It was a comforting thought to Elizabeth, although she realized that angels do not cry. *Almost as if nature is angry that Ted is dead.*

" 'The Lord is my shepherd,' " Morgan began by reading the Twenty-third Psalm.

From his seat, Plomer Hunter surveyed the audience. Emotionally, it was a difficult time for him. Not only did he have to conquer the heartache he felt for the grieving parents, but he had to subjugate his own sense of personal loss, because he had loved Ted as if he were another son.

"I have to talk about how remarkable Ted was. I have to comfort the family. And yet, I want to be instructive," he had told Ruth as he had labored over his message.

Dear God, I pray for the wisdom and the ability to present this message in such a way that it will comfort Frank and Elizabeth and challenge those who have not obeyed the commandments of Your Son. Plomer silently prayed as he approached the podium. He examined the sea of faces in the audience. From the family section, Frank and Elizabeth locked their eyes on him, expectantly.

"I feel greatly honored that you have asked me to have a part in this service," he said directly to the couple. "No greater honor can be bestowed upon a preacher."

Frank acknowledged Plomer with a barely perceptible nod.

"I know of no family for which I have greater respect than this one. I have known Ted for about eleven or twelve years," Plomer said, turning to the audience to continue his eulogy. "I can without the least hesitation say that he was as fine a young man as I have ever known."

He recalled the years he watched Ted mature, the social gatherings in the Morris home, and the recent letter of recommendation he had written at the request of David Lipscomb College.

"That he was greatly liked, I need not to mention. Your presence here today testifies to that fact," he said as a finely honed insight picked up the assembly's silent appreciation.

"I'm sure the greatest tribute that could be paid to him was spoken by his father yesterday when he said, 'If I had been allowed to make a young man just like I wanted him, I would have made him just like Ted.' " The minister paused and looked at Frank and Elizabeth. "I'm sure that Ted felt this same way about his father and mother.

"It does seem that Ted's life was cut very short. It was. But he was not the only young man who was just as fine as he could be and was taken in his youth." He went on to explain that age is relative. "Our Lord Himself was only thirty-three when His life on earth ended. What we many times do not understand is the fact that it is not the length of life that really counts, but the quality that matters most! Maybe Ted's life here was not as long as some others, but in quality it may have been much greater.

"But there is something even more important. As fine as Ted was, I'm quite sure he was not perfect. So he, just like the rest of us, needed a Savior. That Savior is Jesus. Now there are two things that I'm going to say about Ted's life that outweigh all the other things I have said so far. One: Back a number of years ago he heard, believed, and obeyed the glorious gospel of our Lord and Savior. He then and there was saved from sin. He became a member of the Lord's Church." Plomer went on to read Romans 10:17; Hebrews 11:6; Hebrews 5:8,9; and Acts 2:47.

"Then there is a second thing that is also true of Ted's life. He has remained faithful ever since. This, too, is necessary," he explained, reading Revelation 2:10. "Based upon these two truths, we come today with great hope. Hope built upon the Bible. Hope built upon Jesus, the Rock of Ages. Hope in God, the great Creator of this world. If this is not a solid foundation, there is none to be found.

"Finally, we come to pay our respects to Ted and to this family. We have come to help you carry the burden of this hour a little easier," Plomer said, looking at Frank and Elizabeth. "We extend to you our sympathy as best we can. Most of all, we would recommend the One who knows better than we possibly can what you feel this hour and can help you when no one else can.

"The Lord Himself will not leave you but will go with you all the way. His strength will carry you through," he encouraged them.

"Let me remind you again of the words found in Second Samuel 12:15–23," he said, recounting the familiar story of a grieving David praying for the life of his son. Upon the death of the child, David arose, washed, and went about life telling his servants that as long as his son lived, there was hope, but upon death, there was only one recourse. "David realized he could not bring his son back from the dead, but he also knew he could go to him.

"This needs to be our faith today. We believe that Ted is now in a better place. His soul is gone from this body," he explained. "We cannot bring him back, but we can go to him.

"If we have not heard, believed, and obeyed, we need to give serious thought to this while time and opportunity is still ours.

We then need to be faithful unto death, that we might have the crown. May Ted's life be an inspiration unto us all to do what needs to be done to be ready when we, too, must quit the walks of men and meet our Lord in judgment,'' he concluded. ''Let us again pray.''

Perhaps it occurred because of a subconscious association—Frank would always wonder about it—but when the pallbearers carried the casket past his car, to the waiting hearse, he noticed that it was the same deep metallic blue as his automobile. Never again would he see his automobile without a mental flash of Ted's casket.

The funeral cortege stretched for miles as it wound its way through town to Green Hill Memorial Gardens cemetery. The rain had stopped during the funeral service, but the respite was brief. As the procession approached the cemetery, the clouds again gathered; soon there was another pounding rain.

Frank noticed the raw earth spilling out from under the green indoor/outdoor carpet that had been spread under the family tent. It was the only soil that had not been turned into a soggy mire by the pouring rain. Outside the tent, the downpour had caused the cemetery grounds to become spongy, sending up little squashing sounds as the pallbearers bore the casket to the bier. *Elizabeth and I will eventually join Ted here. More importantly, by the time our bodies reach here, we will have already joined him in a glorious home.* That thought gave him a measure of peace.

A few words by Plomer, a prayer, and the graveside service swiftly ended. As long as the family was there, the workmen would not lower the casket into the grave. Shortly the couple sat alone, staring at the coffin as a few mourners talked quietly under the tent. Most of the cars that had overflowed onto the main highway had gone.

"We have to leave," Frank gently told Elizabeth.

She did not say a word, her mind racing. *I don't want to leave. No, I want to leave. I don't ever want to come back here.* But even as she thought it, she knew that she would be back. Even in the depths of her anguish, there was a strange peace here. *I will be back to be with you, Ted.*

"It's over," she said.

Frank was not sure he understood what she meant, but he tried to fashion an answer that would offer hope. "Yes," he paused. "It's over for here, for now; but one of these days there will be a new beginning . . . for all of us."

Elizabeth grasped her husband's hand. "It can't come too soon for me," she said, convinced that he would understand the depths of her misery.

"I know," he said, standing. "We have to leave now."

Elizabeth watched the scene disappear through the back window of the automobile. She could not take her eyes off the metallic blue coffin. When it had disappeared from sight, she reluctantly turned around. In her mind's eye she watched the men lower the coffin into the ground and begin to cover it with dirt.

It's over. My son will be buried in a few minutes. That thought gave her a flutter of panic, but she knew it was from dealing with life on her side of eternity.

From this moment on is the first day of the rest of my life. She visualized a highway stretching across the Kentucky hills and valleys so far that it disappeared from sight. It seemed to her that it stretched into infinity, but at the end of that road stood a smiling Ted, patiently waiting for her. The thought gave her a measure of peace.

Monday
December 27, 1982

The murder case against Tommy Pigage was continued until January 3, 1983.

To say she was surprised would be too much of an understatement, but Ruth Hunter recovered nicely when Judy Anderson identified herself on the telephone.

"I just wanted the Morrises to know that I'm sorry about what happened," Judy said.

"They will be happy to know you called," Ruth said, not knowing exactly what else to say.

There was a awkward pause.

"Tommy is very remorseful," Judy continued before adding, "He even told me that he wished it had been him instead of Ted."

"God knew that Ted was ready and that Tommy wasn't," Judy remembers Ruth telling her. "Ted was a fine Christian young man. If anyone was ready to stand before God, it was him."

"I'd like to talk Mrs. Morris," Judy continued.

"I'm sure she will be glad to talk to you. These are fine Christian people. They are not the kind of people to harbor hate," Ruth said before they hung up.

That night Frank slipped the cassette tape Larry Webb found in Ted's wrecked automobile into their home entertainment center and turned it on before taking a seat next to Elizabeth on the couch. Ted had been listening to the cassette at the time of the crash. Frank tenderly put his arm around his wife as they heard singer Jim Croce finish his haunting ballad "Time in a Bottle." The emotional impact was indescribable. Neither spoke, each lost in his private thoughts. Idly, Elizabeth reached up and took Frank's hand. They sat there for long minutes until the cassette finished and there was no longer any music. Several days of mourning had exhausted their tears, and the emotions of this particular moment were almost too deep for tears.

Finally, Elizabeth broke the silence. "You know that we're going to have to forgive him."

The thought startled Frank. Just a few days before, Elizabeth had bitterly offered to pull the switch on the electric chair, should Tommy Pigage be found guilty of murder. Now she was suggesting forgiveness. It seemed to Frank that the events of the past two days had turned Elizabeth's emotions into quicksilver; they seemed to slither out of his understanding. *Forgiveness? I'm still trying to deal with Ted's death.*

Eventually Frank responded. "I want to show you something," he said, rising from the couch to pick up a large book. "I got it from the Hunters. Jimmy and Sandy had gone to school with this Pigage," Frank explained. "I wanted us to see what the young man who killed our son looks like."

He opened the high school annual and put it in Elizabeth's lap. A dozen or so pictures dotted the page. It took Elizabeth a moment to locate the name *Pigage,* then trace it to the proper picture. Staring back at her was a mustached, chubby-faced teen, his long, shaggy hair wildly framing his head. The tuxedo jacket atop a frilly, stylish dress shirt seemed to accent the boy's absurd appearance.

"A punk!" Frank spat out in disgust as they looked at a picture that to them portrayed a street tough. He could not control the acrid bitterness that flooded his emotions each time he thought of Tommy alive and enjoying life while Ted lay cold in the cemetery.

It was the first time Elizabeth had seen a likeness of Tommy Pigage, and to her, his appearance fit her mental idea of someone who would drive drunk. *Frank's right. He's a punk! Worse than that, he's a murderer.*

It was an ambivalent moment for the Morrises. Their Christian faith advocated forgiveness; their parental love demanded justice. In spite of Elizabeth's outburst a few days before, they both believed they nurtured no real hatred toward Tommy Pigage—at least none that would harm them spiritually. He had killed their son—but there was nothing they could do about that except through mankind's laws. Tommy Pigage would have to answer to God for his unconscionable actions, but they believed that they could find a measure of relief if he answered to man's law, which maintains that driving under the influence, and murder, are punishable by long prison sentences. They secretly nourished the hope that Pigage might even face retribution by death.

Although it assuaged her desire for retribution, Elizabeth Morris was uncomfortable with their growing need for revenge. Their seething, bubbling hatred directly conflicted with their Christianity.

Although Frank and Elizabeth had dedicated their lives to serving God, Christianity had taken on a new reality. It was the key to being with their son again. That realization would come to dominate their lives. *But we'll never make it if we let hatred grow.*

"Father, forgive them, for they know not what they do," Christ had prayed on the cross.

Will Frank and I ever be able to pray that about Tommy Pigage?

Wednesday
December 29, 1982

Judy Anderson had been staring at the telephone for several minutes. About an hour before, she had sat there for more than five minutes, her mind wandering over the events of the past few days. She decided to paint, but she could not keep her thoughts on her work, so she found herself back at the telephone. Finally she dialed the Morris residence.

Elizabeth answered the telephone.

"Mrs. Morris, this is Judy Anderson."

There was a pause on the other end of the line.

"Tommy Pigage's mother."

"Oh?"

"I talked to your minister's wife, and she said it would be all right to call you," Judy continued. *Please don't hang up on me.*

It was an awkward moment for both of them.

"Yes?" Elizabeth waited.

"I wanted to tell you how sorry I am about your son," she said, adding mentally. *I feel so guilty about what happened. Maybe if I had been a better mother. How could you possibly ever approve of me?* "I feel so terrible about it."

"I really can't discuss this right now," Elizabeth said. "I appreciate your calling, and I know this has to be a difficult time for you, also, as a mother. Neither Frank nor I harbor any hatred," Elizabeth added.

"Thank you," Judy said with a slight emphasis on the *you*. "I've already been told that you are not the kind to harbor hate."

BOOK III
Retribution: The Lost Years

Friday
December 31, 1982

"It's been one week since Ted was killed," Elizabeth said after a fitful night. Frank knew. He had been awake and weeping with her as 2:20 came and passed. He knew that stating the obvious sometimes helped.

She knew that they would mark each anniversary as it came. In a matter of hours, it would be the first New Year's, then the first month, the first birthday, the first Mother's Day.

"This has been the hardest week of our lives," she continued as Frank nodded in agreement. "I told her that we didn't harbor hate," Elizabeth added.

"Who?" She had switched subjects on him.

"Him . . . uh, her . . . that Pig . . . ," she stumbled on the name. "Piggy . . . whatever. I told his mother that we didn't harbor any hate," she said softly. "But I can't keep the feeling of hatred from growing inside me. Each day without Ted is a day that something grows, like a shell with a rotten little wet hen in it."

"That sounds normal to me," Frank said. "That boy is not one of my favorite people, either."

The Morris home had been the center of festivities the previous year.

"Ted was here . . . then," Elizabeth said in the middle of their reminiscence, a phrase she would use to mark each milestone.

Saturday
January 1, 1983

"Where is Ted right now?"

It would not be the last time Elizabeth posed that question. It was usually over morning coffee, and it usually indicated that Elizabeth had spent a sleepless night. The couple had tried to sleep late following the joyless New Year's Eve; however, both arose early, and Elizabeth was busy cooking breakfast.

"In paradise," Frank quickly answered. "At least that's where Lazarus was, following his death." Frank referred to the familiar story of the rich man and Lazarus. (While some biblical scholars consider it a parable, others believe that Jesus Christ used a true story as the basis of this simple sermon. The rich man lived a full, sumptuous life, while Lazarus begged at his table. According to Christ, upon his death, the rich man went to a place of punishment, while Lazarus was carried away by angels when he died.)

Elizabeth nodded. She had heard the story; what she sought was reassurance. "Will Ted know me?"

"The rich man could see Lazarus, and knew who he was," Frank patiently explained. He also pointed out that Jesus' apostles recognized the resurrected Lord on several occasions when He appeared to them.

Frank went to his wife, by the stove. "Don't worry. You will know Ted, and he will know you," he said, holding her, stroking her hair. "Try not to worry about it. There is no way you would ever forget him or be unable to recognize him." He added, "And just think, when our time comes, he will be waiting to greet us. We just have to make sure we make it."

"He's just got to know me, Frank."

Elizabeth watched as Plomer Hunter's mother and her husband took down the Christmas tree in the living room. They were careful to preserve the decorations made by a child's tiny hands in grade-school projects. Still others had been crafted at the kitchen table under Elizabeth's watchful eye. All had been added to the tree each year.

That morning, all Ted's packages had been put on the couch by

Elizabeth. She and Frank unwrapped them, putting a pair of sweaters aside for Frank and making a separate pile of gifts that would be returned.

"Frank, we've got to cancel the tennis shoe order." She had just remembered the pair of designer shoes that they had ordered as a special surprise.

At the end of the day, Frank took all the boxes of Christmas decorations into the garage and shoved them deep into the attic. *I'll never use those again,* he promised himself.

Sunday
January 2, 1983

"It's God's will," several well-meaning older women told Elizabeth before worship.

That Ted should die?

"God wanted a rose, so he called Ted home," another said.

But he was my only flower. Perhaps it was the mention of roses, but her mind pictured the bright yellow roses in a vase at home, a gift from her son. *Special flowers. Like him.*

"I know just how you feel." A younger woman holding a small child came by to hug and comfort her.

How can you know? You've never lost a child.

Elizabeth knew these friends were trying to comfort her, but the words only added to her melancholy. A seething indignation rose within her. She tried to subdue it by recalling Frank's words at the funeral home: "It was Satan's will that Ted die, not God's."

She looked at Frank, who was stoically listening to Plomer's sermon.

I wish I could be more like him.

Frank's mind was on the driveway behind their house. It was a hot summer afternoon as father and son went at it one-on-one beneath the basketball goal.

"Why did God do this to me?" Elizabeth tackled the age-old question head-on when they reached home that afternoon.

"It was not God's will," Frank reassured his wife. "It was the will of Satan for Tommy Pigage to do what he did."

Frank paused, articulating each word evenly. "God chose not to work a miracle to deliver Ted." They had both seen the death certificate that said Ted died of hypovolemic shock. The official record listed multiple trauma, cerebral contusion, multiple lacerations, and fracture of the femur. "We both now know that it would have taken a miracle for Ted to live."

"But everyone keeps saying it's God's will."

"They are really not much different from Job's friends who asked him what he had done to make God mad," Frank offered. "His friends did not understand Job's trial. His tribulation came from Satan, who tempted him, not God, who loved him."

At first, Job's friends asked him what he had done to deserve such treatment; finally his wife encouraged him to curse God and die after months of affliction. This misguided advice had played into the hands of Satan, who had asked God for permission to test Job's loyalty. Job steadfastly maintained that he had done nothing to deserve the harsh treatment. He refused to abandon God, who—according to fallible human reasoning—appeared to have abandoned him.

"We have to remain steadfast," Frank encouraged her. "We have to continue to realize that God loves us. He will not visit anything on us that we can't handle."

"I'm not so sure about that," Elizabeth answered.

Monday
January 3, 1983

Tommy Pigage's court appearance to face murder charges was continued until January 10.

The Morrises heard of the delay. Angst would become a way of life for them.

United Parcel Service Center Manager Jim Mohon, Frank's supervisor, accompanied him on his rounds the first day he returned to work.

At home, Frank found Elizabeth surrounded by hundreds of sympathy cards and letters that had flooded their home. There seemed to be a special solace in the long letters from his newly acquired college friends who shared anecdotes. Each new story was a fresh extension of Ted's memory, and she eagerly read them to Frank. Each letter was an affirmation that perhaps his memory would never die.

Frank noticed that Elizabeth was dressed in a pair of Ted's blue jeans and a T-shirt with his name on the back. Her son's high school senior ring still hung around her neck.

Although concerned, Frank believed this obsession with Ted's clothing and possessions would soon pass.

"Elizabeth, I think we should move," he suggested that night.

"Why?" She knew why, but her question was a way to stall while she gathered her thoughts.

"I think it would be best—for both of us. Maybe we should consider getting out of this house," he said. 'It's too full of Ted.''

"That's exactly why we should stay," Elizabeth said. "Everywhere we look, we can see our son."

They were quiet, each considering what the other had to say. Finally Elizabeth spoke from out of the darkness. "There is no way I'll ever leave here," she said quietly.

Friday
January 7, 1983

Elizabeth and her dad, Ted Alverson, had expected to see Ted's killer answer to the law when they saw Tommy Pigage for the first time. Instead, the father and daughter watched as Richard "Kip" Cameron was appointed public defender because Tommy had no funds to mount a defense. A new court date was set for January 21.

Nothing is happening.

Tommy Pigage remained free on his own personal recognizance. Elizabeth felt as if her eyes were boring holes into his back, but he never turned to look at her. He knew she was there, because he had furtively stolen a glance when she did not know it. Officer Breathitt brought a law book back to Elizabeth and explained the charges. Murder charges carry a penalty of twenty years to life. First-degree murder carry a penalty of ten to twenty years. Murder in the second degree is punishable by five to ten years in prison. Reckless homicide charges carry a term of one to five years. Breathitt had filed charges of murder. In Tommy's case, the automobile was considered a weapon, just as if it had been a gun or a knife.

I hope he gets the death penalty, Elizabeth thought, not knowing this was impossible under the law.

Frank discovered Elizabeth busy at work with cellophane tape, glue, scissors, and scrapbook. To one side was a photo album.

"It's a scrapbook . . . about Ted," she answered his quizzical look. Elizabeth shuffled through the papers until she pulled out a card.

"I found this in his room," she said. "It was his last birthday card."

Frank took the card and read it.

Dated March 6, 1982, a message had been written on the back.

> Dear Ted,
>
> I don't know of anything on earth that a person can take more pride in other than their children. And what a joyful blessing for us to have a son like you. If we could have put in a special order to God for everything we wanted a son to be, you've been that & more.
>
> Someday, when you're a parent you will understand the fears & anxieties of parenthood. You have made our job so much easier because you have always been so trustworthy, dependable, loving, thoughtful, sharing, & kind. We appreciate, more than you now realize, your submissive attitude in respecting our wishes. Everything we have asked you to do (or not do), has always been with your best interest at heart. I'm sure you realize that!
>
> We are so proud to have a fine Christian man like you for a son!
>
> I love you very much.

It was signed *Mom,* followed by an ampersand and *Dad* where Frank had also signed.

He looked up with tears in his eyes and, as they had done many times before, they embraced and mourned anew.

Monday
January 17, 1983

Tommy Pigage had had a .28 blood alcohol level, nearly three times the minimum level of a drunk driver. Kentucky considers a person intoxicated who has a .10 reading.

Officer Bob Breathitt expected it to be high, but he was still surprised at the results. The blood had been drawn more than two and one-half hours after the accident, and Tommy's system had been supercharged with adrenaline following the crash.

It would be months before the Morrises would learn of the results.

Restless, Elizabeth drove to Pennyrile Mall early that morning, then waited for the shops to open. It was a routine she would follow in the weeks and months to come, sometimes two and three times a week. Slowly she walked past the Sound Shop. She could not endure the long hours alone at home. *You're still alone, even here,* she told herself as people began to fill the mall's ample walkway, but she welcomed the distraction. Elizabeth passed by a reflective glass, startled to see the image of a woman dressed in blue jeans and T-shirt, dark circles around her eyes. She had barely passed a comb through her hair. For the most part, she successfully hid her true state of mind. An occasional lapse in personal appearance or sloppy housework were rare clues to her turmoil.

Sometimes she would rush home only minutes before Frank arrived after spending the day wandering the mall or visiting Ted's grave. Occasionally, however, Frank would find her in her automobile in the UPS lot awaiting his return, just as she was this day.

Friday
January 21, 1983

"Not guilty, your honor."

Not guilty! The words were like salt in a raw wound. *I'd wring your neck if I could get to you,* Elizabeth silently threatened. Tommy Pigage had just entered his plea in a preliminary hearing where his lawyer waived the murder case on to the grand jury. To Elizabeth, the plea was a personal affront. By that plea, Tommy was absolving himself of guilt in Ted's death. *What you're saying is that if it wasn't your fault, then it was Ted's fault that you killed him.* It was simple to her. There were two cars and two men driving; one of them had to have done something wrong. *And Ted didn't pass out, nor was he on the wrong side of the road.*

Before the session, Tommy's lawyer had explained his strategy to his client. The longer he could delay any trial, the better would be Tommy's chances in court.

"This gives people a chance to cool down, maybe even forget a bit," he had said. "People will not be as upset in the future as they are now, with it still fresh on their minds."

"The longer it's behind me, the cooler it's going to be," Tommy said, acknowledging the lawyer's strategy.

When she returned home, Elizabeth went into Ted's room and lay facedown on his bed. She breathed deeply, seeking his scent. She lay there for hours, quietly weeping, mourning her son's death and the in justice of a court system that appeared to offer little relief to the victims of crime.

She looked around the room, studying every nook and cranny. As each day passed, it became increasingly impos-

sible to concentrate. Her mind leaped from one topic to another.

Where is my cookbook, Ted? Where did you put it? She decided that the cookbook must have been taken, otherwise she
would have found it. *I've searched everywhere.*

She felt the need to possess Ted's last gift more acutely that
day because she had seen his killer that morning. The experience
had so agitated the high-strung woman that her sense of loss was
as keen as the day Ted died. She left the room only a few minutes
before Frank arrived home. A freshly scrubbed face, a brave
smile, and the beginnings of dinner would hide her suffering
psyche.

Thursday
February 3, 1983

Elizabeth found solace by continuing to work on her scrapbook.
She carefully cut out a poem Ted had written January 13, 1980,
when he was sixteen. Jerry Morgan had put it in the current
Southside Church of Christ church bulletin.

> I sit upon this cold hard pew,
>   And I slowly start to nod.
> I wonder why I can't stay awake,
>   When I should be worshiping God.
> I had no trouble staying awake last night
>   As I watched a TV show.
> All that was on was two men in a fight,
>   And after that to bed I would go.
> So now I've decided that I will not
>   Ever stay up late again,

> I'll keep from making the pew a cot
> And I'll be an example to all men.
>
> —Ted Morris

Unable to concentrate for long periods of time, Elizabeth put the scrapbook aside. She decided to iron several of Frank's shirts and a small stack of underclothing. Several hours later she found herself still working on them.

That's strange, I should have finished this long ago. But try as she might, it was difficult to concentrate. Finally she took the underclothing and stacked it into Frank's dresser drawer. Some of it tumbled to one side. *That's good enough,* she thought, closing the drawer.

District Attorney W. E. "Petey" Rogers presented the case to the grand jury. It returned an indictment of second-degree manslaughter, reducing the charge from murder. The lesser charge carried a potential sentence of five to ten years in prison. Also, it was the conventional indictment handed down by Christian County grand juries in murder cases filed as the result of driving under the influence.

Friday
February 4, 1983

As he dressed for work, Frank discovered the normally neat drawer slight askew. It puzzled him. *They must have fallen over when she closed the drawer,* he thought, positive that his super-neat wife would never leave them awry. He did not know about the reduced charge until he turned on the radio as he drove to work.

*   *   *

Elizabeth cut the story out of the newspaper, her hands shaking with fury. How could anyone reduce the charge against that killer? It was plain and simple, a case of murder. He had used a car instead of a bullet.

She pulled the pastepot to her, then decided to get a cup of coffee in the kitchen. Dirty dishes invited her attention. Thirty minutes later she passed through the living room and was startled to see the open pastepot and newspaper clipping.

I forgot all about it. She was amazed. *My, I'm getting forgetful.*

Until the grand jury ruling, Frank and Elizabeth believed they could forgive Tommy Pigage. The ruling polarized their frustration, and as one long day passed into another, the anger and the hatred began to build. Before the grand jury action, it seemed that the laws of the land were working against the victims, not for them. Now they were convinced that they were.

"About the only person who has any rights is the killer," Frank told Elizabeth.

They had hoped that Tommy Pigage would pay the ultimate penalty. Now, not only did he not face the death penalty, but five to ten years in jail would be his maximum sentence.

Life is cheap, Frank barked mentally. And the most galling part of all was that Tommy Pigage was still walking around free. He had not spent one night in jail, yet not one person doubted his guilt.

"All I can think of is that he should die, and how he should die," Elizabeth told Frank. "If ever I see Tommy Pigage on the sidewalk, I'll run over him with my car," she pledged. The legal ballet in the courtroom fed their anger; an anger that would grow into bitter hatred the more the Morrises were frustrated by the court system. The mental numbness that shields injuries had worn off, leaving exposed, irritated nerves.

The wheels of justice seemed slow, but the Morrises were to discover that they had just begun to turn.

That night Elizabeth dreamed of killing Tommy Pigage.

Saturday
February 5, 1983

. . . And when Elizabeth awoke, her consummated hatred evolved into an elaborate fantasy. When the fantasy ended, all she could do was remember Christ's words on the cross: ''Father, forgive. . . .''

I must be the most dreadful person in the world.

Then remorse tinged with guilty mingled with her hatred, and Elizabeth weeped for myriad reasons. From the depths of her anguish came the realization: *Ted would not want this.* The thought only compounded her misery.

This was a time of soul-searching for Judy Anderson. She'd always considered Tommy's drinking a problem, but she had never faced the reality of his addiction, until now. Upon reflection, she even confessed that she suspected Tommy might have been using drugs in high school.

She remembered the sweet young boy who excitedly accepted her marriage to Phelps in 1969. Judy had been divorced from Tommy's father since 1962, when the child was three, and Tommy had seen him only once since then.

Maybe we disappointed him. Tommy had anticipated a more traditional home. It was not many months, however, until relationships between Tommy and Phelps were strained.

Now that Tommy faced a prison sentence, Judy found herself filled with regrets. She believed that dealing with other domestic problems had blinded her to Tommy's needs.

In retrospect, Judy realized she had never talked to Tommy. She had come to realize that children wanted parents to set limits, but she had allowed a free rein.

"If I had been more available," she told Phelps, "if I had tried harder to discuss things with him, his life would have been different."

This is where I failed him.

She was instrumental in persuading Tommy to enter a thirty-day rehabilitation program for alcoholics. His attorney agreed it would help his court case if the judge had proof that he was trying to correct his life. Reluctantly, he entered the VOLTA program.

Sunday
February 6, 1983

Frank stopped by Ted's room on the way downstairs. He could hear Elizabeth busy in the kitchen. He knew that very little had been touched. If Ted were to come whistling into the room, he would find it unchanged. His mother had taken thin plastic and carefully wrapped everything but the bed. A beach ball rested in the center of it. If Elizabeth wanted to keep this room as a museum to Ted, then she could. He had heard that sometimes this happened.

Frank decided to check the titles of books Ted had put on a shelf. Frank had always believed that he could take the measure of a man by his reading. He followed the titles, which ranged from fiction to Bible study books, Ted's Bible, and a book tucked across the top of the other books, spine turned toward the back, pages outward.

Wonder what this is? Frank thought, lifting it out of its place.

A cookbook? Frank knew immediately what he had found. He carefully replaced it.

"Elizabeth," he called, barely able to conceal his pleasure. "Would you come up here?"

"Have you checked Ted's bookcase?" he asked her when she entered. *Let her find it.* Let her take it out. Let her discover the special place where Ted had hidden it in plain sight.

"What for?" she said.

"Just look," he answered.

She caught his sense of excitement, quickly scanned the titles, then turned to Frank, questioning.

"Look at the top."

Elizabeth looked again, spotted the book lying backwards across the top. "It's here." She said it so softly, so full of wonder. She never thought to look above the other books. *He was so clever; he hid it where I would never look.*

"Take it down. It's your gift . . . from your son," Frank said, his voice breaking.

Gingerly she lifted it from its place and caressed it from top to bottom, then read the words, *Party Time in Kentucky*. It was a cookbook sold by the American Cancer Society, Kentucky Division, to raise funds.

Tears streamed down her cheeks as she gently held it. For nearly two months she had pined for this book. Finally, she had given up. She had assumed something had happened to it, only to discover it safe in Ted's room.

Wednesday
February 9, 1983

Tommy was surprised to discover a measure of relief in the VOLTA program. Five or six chemical abusers were assigned to a discussion group under the direction of a counselor. At the end of the thirty-day program, Tommy believed he had made progress. In later years, however, he would look back on the program as only the beginning. "It takes a lot longer than a month or two for people to get their lives in good shape," he would say. "After someone goes through one month of this program, he enters the most dangerous time. It takes that long just to dry out. You are very susceptible to going back to your old ways. Three months would have been more helpful."

Thursday
February 10, 1983

District Attorney Rogers disqualified himself from prosecuting the case. His wife was Phelps's child from a previous marriage, and she could be considered Tommy's stepsister. A special prosecutor from the state attorney general's office was requested.

For the second time, Frank broached the subject of moving; Elizabeth remained firm. A move would do more harm than good. After Frank left, Elizabeth looked up the story of the blind man who had been healed in John 9. She was still wrestling with the possibility that Ted's death had in some way been a punishment for her.

What did I do? she prayed. *What did I do to make You do this to me?*

Frank had prepared a sermon based on this chapter. The man had been blind since birth. Christ was asked who sinned, this man or his parents. Christ pointed out that neither had sinned to cause this affliction. As in the case of Job, not all things that happen are due to a person's actions. And not everything that happens is God's will. Job's temptations bore that out. Satan wanted to tempt Job, not God. Satan rained death and destruction on this godly man.

But it is like I'm being punished for doing right. I've been faithful. I've been involved in church work, Elizabeth reasoned. *I know that I'm not perfect, but I have tried to please God.*

She sat there for a long time, considering her situation. She could come to only one conclusion: *It is so hard to live without Ted.*

Monday
February 14, 1983

Tommy waived an arraignment hearing. It was not an unusual legal maneuver, but when anxious parents are awaiting equity, it becomes yet another meaningless obstacle on the road to justice. The next court date was set for April 7.

Elizabeth picked up her mother, and the two rode to the cemetery. Snow and rain and wind had melded the dirt clods into a smooth mass of bald soil. Grass would be sodded in the coming spring. A marker bearing Ted's name had been positioned at the head of the grave. Floy Alverson kneeled by the grave site. She leaned over to touch the marker, gently rubbing its cold surface, often tracing Ted's name. Elizabeth kneeled on the opposite side and prayed. Sometimes she just talked to Ted.

She told him the news of the town, how much she missed him, and how much she loved him. This day, she laid a single rose at the headstone. It was Valentine's Day, her first without him.

These visits became a regular ritual. Sometimes the women made several trips a week.

Monday
February 28, 1983

Elizabeth A. Myerscough, an assistant attorney general in the state office, was named special prosecutor. The Morrises had had precious little contact with prosecutors; now the people responsible for obtaining justice for their son's death were in Frankfort, two hundred miles away.

Saturday
March 5, 1983

Tommy Pigage was released from the thirty-day alcoholic rehabilitation program. He went straight to his apartment after stopping for a bottle of bourbon. But he surprised himself; he did not take a drink.

I've been four weeks without a drink. Why do this?

He poured the glassful of liquid down the drain, screwed the top on the bottle, and put it in a cabinet, and went out to look for a job.

He spent the evening sober.

Monday
March 21, 1983

County Circuit Judge Alfred A. Naff signed an order changing the trial date from April 7 to April 27.

"They've been to court or set court dates so many times I'm about to lose count," Frank told Elizabeth. "It looks like we will never have justice."

You might as well resign yourself to the fact that you will never get it. Once again, it appeared that the courts protected the criminals. Frank could not help but wonder what happened to the spirit exhibited by the original law officers who filed the murder charges.

Tommy had been unable to find a job. Bored, unable to cope with his building remorse over Ted's death, Tommy found release the same way he had since he was sixteen: He went to the local convenience store, bought a six-pack of beer, and began a pattern of drinking himself into an alcoholic slumber each night.

Wednesday
April 20, 1983

Special Prosecutor Myerscough requested a continuance until June 6 because expert witnesses were unavailable.

Elizabeth spent the day walking the mall. She spotted a little doll that looked lifelike. Tiny hands reached out for love; gentle blue eyes seemed to be calling out from the carefully crafted head.

I've got to have that baby, she thought. *No, Frank would kill me.* Then, just as quickly, *It's what I want. I deserve it.*

Resolved, she walked into the children's toy shop. She held the doll, reveling in the thought of a child's love, remembering Ted's long-ago gurgling. The desire to have a baby to love was a burning ache in the pit of her stomach.

No. It would be the wrong thing for me, right now, she thought, replacing the doll on the display shelf.

"Thank you," she said. "I'll be back."

She would come back several times to visit this toy shop, always pledging to herself that she would buy the doll *when the time was right.*

Frank found his underwear thrown into the dresser drawer, shorts and T-shirts intermingled, nothing ironed.

Monday
June 6, 1983

A backlog of litigation forced another delay in trying the case. A new date was set for September 12.

Puzzled, Elizabeth held the batch of letters she had just discovered. Bills. Frank had given them to her several days before to be mailed, but Elizabeth had forgotten. When Frank came in that evening, she gave him the bills. "I can't seem to remember to mail them," she said.

Frustrated at first, Frank accepted them. Elizabeth had become very forgetful. Even her comprehension seemed to wander. Sometimes he would have to tell her something several times before she could understand the simplest request.

That night after dinner, Frank's stomach was unsettled, even painful, but he dismissed it as bloating; something he had eaten must not have agreed with him.

Sunday
September 11, 1983

As Elizabeth continued to sink into despondency, it became almost a game to go to church and hide her real feelings. Everyone marveled at how well she had adjusted to Ted's death. They did not see the long, rambling walks in the malls or the disheveled home that had once been so spotless. Elizabeth hid her inability to concentrate behind a mask. Each Sunday morning she would awaken and put on her mask. *All secure, all's right with the world.* At church, helpful friends would praise her.

"I couldn't do as well as you have" was a common refrain.

Inside, Elizabeth felt rotten. Not only did she believe that her spiritual life was hypocritical, but her public persona was a mask hiding a woman on the verge of a nervous breakdown. Like her dream, her real life began to slow down, each simple task taking more and more time.

Monday
September 12, 1983

Each worried about the other, yet each reserved a private place for grief in the mistaken belief that the best interests of the other were being served. As a couple they reached out to each other, sharing many tender moments; yet each seemed unable to lift the other out of creeping emotional quicksand.

To Elizabeth, Frank was stoic, strong. The strength was there even during the vulnerable times when they would talk about Ted and hold onto each other and cry. Frank had no outward signs of grief.

Unknown to her, he would slip into Ted's room to sit and think. He worried that it was mentally unhealthy but frankly admitted to himself: *I do like being here.*

Meanwhile, Elizabeth tried to hide her eccentric actions. *I don't want people to think I'm crazy.*

Tommy Pigage's trial date was rescheduled January 23, 1984.

Frank walked in to find Rose Jeffcoat Wyatt a captive audience. She was surrounded by memorabilia, Elizabeth's cherished album in her lap. Although it was not the first time Rose had seen this album, Elizabeth was turning each page, commenting on a poem or a card or a picture. Rose patiently made the appropriate comment.

It was not just Rose—anyone who walked through the Morrises' front door was invited to view the album.

"You're going to drive people away," Frank said gently after Rose left.

Elizabeth looked at him, questioning.

"I know it is important that you keep Ted's memory alive, but you're going to drive people away with that album."

Elizabeth stifled an angry reply. She knew Frank was right. She could not let her desire to keep Ted's memory alive drive their friends away. Still, she wanted her friends to know how much he loved her, how special Ted was. *But at what price?* she asked herself. "You're right," she said quietly. She put the scrapbook away, and it seldom came out after that.

Saturday
December 24, 1983

It had been a year since Ted had died. Elizabeth marked the first anniversary by retrieving six garbage bags from the kitchen. Once upstairs in Ted's room, she began to take the linen off his bed. It was the first time it had been removed since Ted's death.

The mother hugged the bedspread, filling her nostrils with its scent. But there was a slight disappointment. The distinctive musk that had first been there was gone. Elizabeth stuffed the bedspread into one bag and tied it closed, very tightly. Sheets and pillows followed, until she had five bags all tightly tied. She carried them downstairs. When Frank came in that night, he shoved them next to the Christmas decorations in the attic.

Sunday
December 25, 1983

Frank and Elizabeth departed on what would become an annual trip to Florida during the Christmas holidays.

Wednesday
January 11, 1984

The Morrises, Tommy Pigage, and Judith Oldham Anderson gave depositions in the case of Frank E. Morris, individually, and Frank E. Morris, administrator of the estate of Ted M. Morris, deceased, vs. Thomas Pigage and Judith O. Anderson. The Morrises had filed a civil suit, seeking damages in Ted's death.

The Morrises testified concerning their son's educational and work history, while Judy acknowledged that Tommy was given use of the Buick. Tommy's testimony was composed of a series of objections by defense lawyer Kip Cameron. Although Tommy had already claimed he had little recall of the accident, Cameron refused to let him discuss the evening, on the grounds that his deposition might tend to incriminate him.

Sunday
January 22, 1984

At Frank's insistence, Elizabeth invited the Hunters to Monday-night dinner.

"I'm not sure I can do this," she told Frank.

"We need to be around people," he said. "Especially you. You've almost become a recluse."

The Hunters readily accepted. Like Frank, they thought it would be good for Elizabeth to entertain.

Monday
January 23, 1984

A pretrial conference was set for May 18, 1984, and the trial date was set for May 29, 1984. Finally, Tommy Pigage would face a jury.

The pain was so intense that Frank had to pull to the side of the road on the drive home. His gut felt as if coals of fire were surging through them. The severe pain passed in a few moments, but was followed with diarrhea.

Plomer and Ruth arrived shortly before six o'clock. A flustered Elizabeth met them at the door. The table had not been set, the meal was only half-prepared, she had just finished cleaning the house, and had not changed clothes. Their arrival was the high point of the evening. Dinner was several hours late. It was a miserable social disaster for Elizabeth, no matter that the Hunters were good friends, almost family.

"Oh, Frank, what's the matter with me?" Elizabeth cried out for help. "I can't even get a simple meal together."

Friday
April 27, 1984

Kip Cameron, Tommy's court-appointed attorney, filed a motion to withdraw from the case, since he was entering private practice. The motion was granted and a date set for the judge to appoint a new public defender. Another frustrating delay.

Lou Ann Rogers would not let Elizabeth ignore her. She rang the doorbell until her friend answered.

"Read this," she said, shoving a copy of *People Weekly* magazine into Elizabeth's hands. It was open to a story about a mother's battle against drunk driving. "Have you ever heard of MADD? Is coffee made?"

When Elizabeth finished the article, Lou Ann challenged her. "Why don't we start a chapter here?"

For the first time in months, Elizabeth heard something that really interested her. Over the next few weeks, the two women would be joined by Rose Jeffcoat Wyatt. They researched the idea by contacting Loretta Little, president of the MADD chapter in Lexington. She was invited to speak at an organizational meeting in May. The three passed out leaflets urging people to attend.

Tuesday
May 8, 1984

Joel R. Embry III was named Tommy's new public defender. There would be another delay: The attorney needed time to become familiar with the case.

Frank's stomach pain became so intense that he finally visited the family doctor, who discovered that Frank suffered from ulcerated colitis. The doctor noted that this chronic condition is often coupled with severe stress.

Frank and Elizabeth decided to take another soothing trip to Florida. Not only would it give Frank a chance to relax, but the couple did not want to be in Hopkinsville during the Mothers Against Drunk Driving organizational meeting. They feared it might hurt the case against Tommy Pigage. Before the Morrises left, however, they paid for a hotel room for the guest speaker, and Elizabeth left a corsage. Approximately fifty people attended the organizational meeting, including Circuit Judge Edwin White. Debbie Dunn was elected president; Rose would serve as secretary. It would be the only meeting the judge could attend as a spectator. Fearful of conflict of interest between the organization and his official duties, the judge elected to attend future meetings only in an official capacity.

Tuesday
May 15, 1984

Upon returning from Florida, Frank and Elizabeth plunged into work with MADD. The dedicated group would receive a charter within a few months.

The parents found solace in a letter-writing campaign against the lenient treatment of drunk drivers in Kentucky, where punishment is at the discretion of judges. Their efforts would be part of a statewide drive that eventually helped MADD push through several new laws that mandated a jail term when a drunk driver injured anyone.

Friday
July 6, 1984

Myerscough asked Judge White to set a new trial date. Now it seemed to the Morrises that the "good guys" were delaying justice.

Shelva Biggs telephoned Elizabeth. Her daughter, Renee, had been killed by a drunken driver, August 9, 1977.

"I know how you feel," she told Elizabeth, who knew that this special woman did understand. Her words had a special meaning to the still-grieving mother. The women talked for more than an hour as Elizabeth fired question after question at her.

I'm not losing my mind. These are natural feelings, Elizabeth concluded when she hung up the telephone. It helped her to know that there would be an end to her depression. It was also the first time she could talk to someone about marital intimacy. It was as if her joy in living had died the night her son was killed.

"Everything will pass," Shelva had reassured Elizabeth. "Just keep fighting."

Since Elizabeth had become fearful that she would never be able to concentrate or function normally, Shelva's unsolicited telephone call eased her despondency.

Thursday
July 12, 1984

Judge White set a trial date for September 18. Now Tommy Pigage would face a jury. The Morrises believed that the man who killed their son finally would go to jail for what he had done.

Elizabeth was named MADD's monitor of the court system in Todd County. Each week she would go to court, watch the proceedings, and silently take notes.

"Not much is happening to DUI offenders," she reported to Frank. It had been her observation that many drivers were charged, but through legal maneuvering, the charges were reduced to a lesser offense, and when they returned to court on new DUI charges, it would once again be a first-time offense. "Some of these courts have people who have been in court for DUI many times, yet they can still drive in their counties."

Elizabeth found the court results disheartening. Slowly she began to slip back into a deep depression.

Tuesday
September 11, 1984

Elizabeth Myerscough telephoned. Tommy Pigage's trial was to begin September 13. She requested a personal meeting the next day; there had been some developments she wanted to discuss with them before the trial date.

Wednesday
September 12, 1984

Tommy Pigage would not be tried for second-degree manslaughter. There would be no trial for Ted's death.

Frank and Elizabeth were astounded to learn that behind-the-scenes maneuvering between Tommy's attorney, the judge, and the special prosecutor had resulted in a plea bargaining that would give Tommy Pigage a probated sentence if he pled guilty to the charge of second-degree manslaughter.

"This is totally unacceptable to me," Frank told Beth Myerscough when she finished briefing the couple in their home. "In effect, you're saying that he's getting off and nothing has happened to him."

Myerscough pointed out that Tommy would be under supervision.

"He would be in prison," Elizabeth reasoned.

"His only punishment is to plead guilty." Frank pressed the point. "He hasn't spent a day in jail."

This is mind-boggling. Pigage pleads guilty. The judge sentences him to ten years in jail, then probates that to five years, Frank thought. *Where's justice for Ted's death?*

Aloud, Frank added, "I don't like the bargain that was made. Do you really consider this to be punishment?"

"I'm sorry, Mr. Morris, but the deal has been cut. It's the best we can do, and that's the way it is going to be." Frank remembers Elizabeth Myerscough's businesslike approach to the deal as she added, "You really don't have any say in it."

"No. I'm only the victim," he shot back. "My son . . . my family . . . my wife. I guess we really don't count."

That night the old familiar pain returned to his gut. Elizabeth was uncharacteristically silent.

Thursday
September 13, 1984

It was always the same.

Chilling winter winds nipped at Elizabeth Morris's hair as

she stepped out of the house. A few rust-colored leaves whirled across the driveway, barely visible in the early morning darkness.

Only a few more weeks until Christmas. It was a bleak thought. What had once been a season of joy would be an exercise in futility this year.

Don't think, she cautioned herself.

She had to hurry, or she would be late for work, but she always paused to look at their house, their two-story dream home that Frank had lovingly built on a part of her father's farm in the Kentucky countryside. Within its walls a child had been nurtured through infancy, then tenderly disciplined through childhood, and carefully guided through adolescence, until the parents had happily realized that Ted Morris had been successfully reared into young adulthood. It was a home brimming with happy memories, until *that* Christmas.

Elizabeth felt the tears. It was a moment suspended in time. It always was. Light and shadows.

Christmas Eve last year. No it could not be last year, Ted was already gone last year. It was on Christmas Eve two years ago that eighteen-year-old Ted had become a family memory. *Has it been only two years?* She and her son had lingered in the living room before he went to work. Back then, but an emotional eternity removed, their conversation had been a trivial moment in life. Later it became a precious memory that she would often replay in her mind. Nothing unique had marked that moment.

Except it was the last time you saw him alive, she thought.

She felt that there should have been something special about those final few minutes, but there was not, so she did not have a final embrace, a final smile, a final "I love you."

"I'm gone." How often did his customary parting still ring in her ears? "I'm gone," and he had walked through the door and into her memory.

How was I to know how real those words would become before the sun would rise the next day? she wondered.

She looked at the door, the same door that Ted had walked out and to his death at the hands of a drunken driver. Did the door seem to have a halo of red? or was it her imagination? a trick of the early-morning sun?

She never could figure it out.

Now the car keys felt like lead weights, her arm struggling to lift them to the car door. This simple task took all her concentration as she inserted the key, twisted it, swung the door back, and settled into the driver's seat. She knew that if someone was watching her, her actions would appear normal. But Elizabeth also knew that since Ted's death, nothing was normal anymore. She had lived in slow motion since the night she and Frank had received the telephone call. Life was now an ordeal. An endless second-after-second remembrance of Ted, his face constantly before hers, little snatches of memory—sometimes the most insignificant incidents—balm for her indescribable pain, but only for the briefest instant.

In the past year she had discovered only two things could possibly bring lasting relief: revenge and suicide.

Either or both.

Somehow she got the keys into the ignition; she always seemed to be able to do that. When she backed the car out of the driveway, Elizabeth saw a shadow at a window.

Ted?

No! But his distinctive shadow seemed to always be on the window to his room. Every time she backed the car up like this, she always thought she saw Ted.

Now she was truly in slow motion, and despite the slug-
gish progress of the world around her, it seemed that within
a heartbeat she was driving down Canton Pike, and there was
his apartment! She did not come this way and down this particular street on purpose; she had to drive this way to go to
work, she reminded herself. By now her heartbeat was in her
ears. Ka-thump. Ka-thump. Her breathing became rapid and
shallow, her senses keenly alert, her hands trembled on the
steering wheel, her foot eased the accelerator forward, the car
picked up speed. She steadied her nerves. What if he did not
walk out?

But she knew he would.

And he did.

He stepped into the glaring headlights of her car, his face
distorted by surprise.

Just as Ted was surprised, Elizabeth thought.

Suddenly her world exploded into a contradictory existence that whirled at an exaggeratedly rapid pace one moment
and in slow motion the next; her intellect told her it was impossible, but to her senses the sensations of fast and slow
seemed to happen at the same time. The car shot off the road,
chasing him across the sidewalk and into the yard. Just as he
was about to get away from her she would gun the automobile
in front of him, turning him as a fine-tuned quarter horse works
livestock. He appeared to run in slow motion and it would seem
as if he could run for miles, herky-jerky and always out of
reach, and she could barely keep up with him, her motions
leaden; but she sensed that the automobile never left the apartment yard.

She ran back and forth, enjoying the sheer power of control
until finally Elizabeth wheeled the automobile across the lawn to

pin him against a telephone pole, the bumper against his knees, the hood touching his belly.

Then she slammed the accelerator to the floorboard.

The scream of anguish shook her awake. Frank looked at the clock. It was two in the morning. He took his anguished wife into his arms.

"The dream again?" He knew the answer before he asked. Weeks had passed after Ted's death before it had started, and now it coincided with developments in Pigage's court case. On this day their son's murderer would be sentenced.

"Everything that is happening is to his benefit, not Ted's or ours," Elizabeth whispered in the darkness. Resentment choked her voice as she added, "I want him in jail."

"So do I," Frank acknowledged the acrimonious wish.

"Oh, Frank," she moaned.

They lay in the quiet, each enshrouded in a private misery, each trapped by a hatred that only seemed to grow with each memory of Ted and the thought of Tommy Pigage walking free.

"We keep waiting for relief, but there's not any. We keep waiting for justice, but there's none." She rolled over to look into his face. "Every time he goes to court his lawyers get the trial postponed.

"The court won't execute him," she said with a wry laugh, almost a bark. "They won't even put him in jail."

They lay quietly, each submerged in thought.

Finally Elizabeth added: "Somehow, for us, for Ted, we've got to end it, but I don't know how."

Frank just hugged her more tightly.

"I feel like a whited sepulcher. Like the hypocrites in the Bible, who Christ said were like tombs; pretty and white on the outside, full of dead men's bones on the inside,'' Elizabeth searched for an explanation of her personal demons.

All she could do was repeat the comparison.

"I feel like a whited sepulcher. Everyone at church thinks I'm handling this so well."

Elizabeth knew that to the world around them—including fellow Christians—they appeared to be devoted Christians who were handling the loss of their son with grace and dignity. It was an image they struggled to maintain, while privately, their souls festered with malignity.

"You're just a normal person," he reassured her, but her description of herself caused him to carefully select each word. He did not want to add to her anguish. "No, you're not a normal person, you're much better than that. I've never known you to be anyone but a person filled with love.

"You've. . . ."

There's a better word.

"We've. . . ." he began again, with a slight pause to let Elizabeth realize he had changed person to include himself. "We've suffered a great loss."

He continued to comfort his grieving wife, longing for the magic words to ease not only her grief, but his sorrow as well. Their agony threatened to consume both of them. They had remained close in all things, but one. At first, sharing the grief that accompanied Ted's death had been natural, and they still shared their mourning, but after nearly twenty-four months each had isolated a portion of private thoughts, and these musings had created a private hell that they could not share, would not share for fear of inflicting even greater grief on the other.

Frank was distraught over Elizabeth's actions, some he even found to be irrational. But he realized that sometimes he was unreachable, himself, as he cultivated solace in silence with a stoic attitude that stood firm in the face of tragedy. However, they did share a common foe. Nearly two years after Ted's death, their grief had grown into a bitter hatred for Tommy Pigage.

"But I think things you'd never believe," Elizabeth interrupted his thoughts.

"I might."

"Deep, terrible thoughts that have nothing to do with dreams," she added, hinting at an appalling secret. "Thoughts that fill me with shame."

"We've suffered the greatest loss parents could suffer." He knew of nothing else to tell her. "You're a kind, gentle person; the hatred will pass."

At least I pray to God that it will, he added silently.

After a few minutes the tears dried, and Elizabeth rested her head on Frank's shoulder. They lay quietly, each submerged in private agony, until she could tell from his breathing that he had escaped the present anguish through sleep.

She nestled her head on his shoulder and closed her eyes. This time there was no dream. Elizabeth fantasized herself behind the wheel of her automobile. Tommy Pigage's eyes were wide with terror at the realization of pending retribution, even death. In her mind's eye Elizabeth Morris slammed the accelerator to the floorboard, and the automobile rammed forward. She heard his knees snap, saw the hood crumpling against his belly. A scream ripped out of his twisted mouth. Across the crinkled hood she stared straight into his eyes. This was her special moment, and Tommy Pigage died the most horrible, slow death she could imagine.

She dropped off to sleep with a smile on her lips.

But when she awoke, all she could think of was suicide.

Elizabeth could not remember the first time she had considered suicide. It was an option born out of what seemed to be unbearable grief. Yet it was an option that violated the very integrity of her religious beliefs.

It's time. It was not the first time she had made that decision. On several other occasions, she had decided it would easier to die than to live without her son, but it had only been a mental exercise.

Today was different. She had decided that she wanted to be buried beside Ted. It would be a permanent way of dealing with her grief. After making up the bed, she went to her closet, reached into the back and took out her navy blue suit, still in the dry cleaner's plastic cover. She wanted to be buried in the same clothes that she had worn to Ted's funeral—that seemed a fitting tribute to her son. She retrieved the white blouse that was next to the suit.

She laid them side-by-side on the bed. No, that was not right. She took the blouse out of the bag and put it under the blue jacket. That way there would be no mistake.

Next, she selected underclothing, disappointed that she could not remember what she had worn the day of the funeral, and put them on the bed, smoothing the wrinkles.

The flowers! Startled. *I almost forgot the flowers.* Elizabeth rushed downstairs to get a shadow box of yellow roses hanging amid a picture gallery of Ted she had carefully arranged on the wall that formed the base of the stairway. He had given her the silk roses as a gift. A few months after his death she had had several of them framed and instructed Frank: "When I die, I want this opened and the roses put in my hands. I want to be buried with them.''

Satisfied that everything was in order after placing the framed flowers on the bed, she retrieved the twenty-two-caliber pistol that she had hidden. The first time she had contemplated suicide, she had taken the pistol from Frank's hiding place, then stashed it in her own cache.

Prepared, she went into Ted's room, carrying her diary. Elizabeth planned to telephone the funeral home only seconds before she pulled the trigger. By the time attendants arrived, they would find her dead. Frank would not have to discover her body. Her clothes would be laid out. All Frank had to do was bury her beside Ted.

She opened the diary, balancing it on her knees while using the pistol barrel to mark her place. It was all there. Nearly two years of agony. Months of growing bitterness, each day more galling than the one before as her life slid into a despondent morass of depression. Nearly two years without justice; nearly two years without Ted that now had culminated in her decision to commit suicide.

Nearly two years had been ripped from the pages of her life. That day's page lay blank before her. She knew there would be no one to complete it. That day Tommy Pigage was supposed to enter court and plead guilty. It had been made crystal clear the night before that there was nothing they could do about it. Her faith in the legal system had been exhausted. She knew there was no justice. *The drunken scum will continue to be free, but I will not be forced to be here to watch it.*

One last thing.

Dear God, she prayed. *I know that You know how much I miss Ted. I know that You know how I long to see him, to touch him, to talk to him. I know he is with You.*

I know that what I am about to do is wrong, but I know

that You will understand, she reasoned. *You don't want me to suffer. You don't want me to go long years without seeing my son.*

So if I kill myself, You'll forgive me, because You understand. You're almighty. You can do anything—forgive any sin.

To Elizabeth's surprise, part of her mind interjected a thought into the prayer. *He can forgive, but will He forgive a deliberate sin for which you cannot repent and ask forgiveness because you no longer exist on this earth?*

He can do anything, she argued. *I'm asking forgiveness before I do it.*

Caught up in the moment, she forgot her plans to telephone the funeral home and raised the pistol to her head, holding it with both hands. At that instant her senses were heightened. It was as if she could feel everything around her, as if she could feel Ted's very presence in this room, waiting for her to pull the trigger. *I'll be with you soon, Son.* The cool metal of the gun, her ragged breathing, the trigger under her finger as she gently began to apply pressure—all flowed into her stream of consciousness. Strangely, she never felt more alive than at this moment of pending death.

Her mind went back to her prayer. *You know how I feel. You know that I'm justified in this. I know You'll forgive me.*

She found herself repeating the phrases, over and over. One gentle tug, one split second, and her suicide would be completed.

But if you're not forgiven for this, you will never see Ted again.

There was no more frightening thought than this. *Where did it come from?* She realized that her intellect had overcome the impulse of the moment. Years of Bible study had taught her that she could not receive forgiveness for a sin before it was committed. In her desperation, she was trying to bargain with her Creator to serve her own aching desires.

O God, help me! she screamed in silent anguish.

For long seconds, Elizabeth hung between choosing life or death.

You want to see Ted again, her common sense told her. *This way you run a risk. Otherwise, you endure long years of loneliness, but you keep the faith, you receive a reward.*

Although all her senses were heightened, it was not until she felt the barrel of the pistol pressed against her throbbing temple that she understood the veracity of her mental debate.

I can't do it. Distress was mingled with relief and consternation. She slammed the pistol into her lap, now afraid she might accidentally kill herself.

Elizabeth shook violently. "What have I almost done?" she said aloud. Startled, she realized that she had almost killed herself in her son's room. *Ted would never have wanted me to kill myself. . . .* She let the thought trail off. When the trembling stopped and calm returned, she bowed her head. She realized that self-destruction would never please God. *Father, forgive me,* she prayed.

She replaced the gun in its secret place. The pistol would keep her options open. But, somehow, she believed it would never again tempt her, because she had teetered on the edge and had come to an understanding of herself. It chilled her to acknowledge that she had almost taken the devil's option.

Years later she would find it odd to realize that during all her preparations to make the immediate aftermath and reality of her suicide as easy on Frank as possible, she had never considered what would have been the most devastating blow to her husband: life without her.

Elizabeth looked at the clock on Ted's desk. It was nearly time for the hearing. She grabbed the telephone, dialing furiously. "Rose, I'll meet you there," she said.

She had come close to the unthinkable. Now her mind was clear. If it was the last thing she ever did, Elizabeth Morris was going to see Tommy Pigage behind bars.

"I have to admit to myself, and to everyone, that I have done something wrong. I thought I could fool everyone, but those parents are always there, always a reminder, no matter where I go. I'm tired. I'm frustrated. I don't want the case to be held over again." Tommy Pigage was in a reflective mood that afternoon before facing the judge. It had taken him more than two weeks to reach the decision to admit guilt after the plea bargain was offered. The prosecution would ask for a ten-year prison sentence, but because it was Tommy's first offense, they would agree to a ten-year sentence in which Tommy would be free on five years' probation. The judge would set a date within a few weeks for formal sentencing, at which time he would set the conditions of probation. After nearly two years of legal maneuvering, Tommy's attorneys had negotiated a light sentence. The plan to let the incident cool down had appeared to work; only the parents were still hot over the death of their son.

"Guilty, your honor."

Both Frank and Elizabeth had believed they would never hear those words. It was an emotional moment that defied description. Ted's parents had hoped that those words would relieve nearly two years of frustration, but they did not. Although the guilty plea was pleasing to their ears, it was confusing to their intellects. All their lives, they had believed that justice was a simple process. From childhood on, they had been taught a basic tenet: Guilt meant punishment. Now that they faced the cold, hard reality of the American legal system, the Morrises could not help but wonder if guilt really did mean that the perpetrator would receive adequate punishment.

Finally, their nemesis had admitted guilt, but plea bargaining had reduced retribution yet again. The possibilities had gone from the distinct chance of life in prison to probation. Where was the punishment? And while the Morrises had hoped for execution, that was never a legal option. Frank and Elizabeth felt as if the whole system favored the lawbreakers, with little compassion for the victims. What was transpiring before their eyes seemed to confirm those beliefs.

Except for Ted's death, this was the low point of their lives. According to the agreement, it was possible that Pigage would not spend one night in prison, but the judge could rule that Tommy spend every other weekend in jail for the next two years.

Judge White set an October 26 court date for his final ruling.

Bitter to the point of tears, Frank clutched Elizabeth's hand as his son's killer walked from the courtroom.

He won! Frank felt the bile rise in his throat; his stomach throbbed from the tension. *The prosecutors did exactly what they said they were going to do. Ted's death will never truly be avenged.*

"Come on," Elizabeth told him. "I have an idea. We've got work to do, and we've only got a little over a month. It won't be what we want, but maybe we can make Tommy Pigage's life as miserable as ours has been."

Rose joined the couple as they walked out the door, and when Frank learned what the women had in mind, he was amazed. If the angry parents could not have his life, then the Morrises would get their pound of flesh from Tommy Pigage.

Thursday
October 4, 1984

My mouth is so dry I could spit cotton.

Shy by nature, Elizabeth always found it hard to speak in public, but on this night she would have fought for the opportunity to stand before a special meeting of Mothers Against Drunk Driving.

"Judge Edwin White is considering Tommy Pigage's future," she began. "I believe we can influence his decision, since the judge has sole authority to set the boundaries of his sentence."

She could tell that the thought intrigued each member of the audience.

"Most of you have already gone through what happened to Frank and me," she continued, referring to the recent court hearing. "You have had years to consider what might be proper punishment for someone like Tommy Pigage.

"Now . . . ," Elizabeth paused to look at the audience. How many times had she mourned with many of these members? How many seminars? How many speeches? They had stood shoulder to shoulder against injustice.

"Now is your chance . . . our chance. I believe that Judge White will listen to us," she continued earnestly. "Let's give him a list of suggestions. Let's help him give Tommy Pigage some of the punishment he deserves.

"This is a country of laws, but frankly, for two years it seems to me that those laws just haven't worked for us. Ted's killer runs free—he enjoys the benefits of freedom, which were provided by the law—while the family mourns its loss and wonders if there will ever be justice.

"Now is our chance to help mete out justice. I want Ted to rest in peace in my mind," she concluded. "If we succeed, I think it will help not only Frank and me, but all of us."

Friday
October 19, 1984

Circuit Judge Edwin White carefully studied the letter that crossed his desk that morning. A strong-willed man, he was determined to run his court his way, but he was open to communication. The letter written by Rose Wyatt intrigued him. By law, the judge was required to consider probation before taking any other action.

Thursday
October 25, 1984

That night Elizabeth came into Frank's arms.

"Pray Frank, just pray aloud."

They both knew that the next day would be a pivotal point in their lives.

Friday
October 26, 1984

The Christian County courthouse is a historic structure. It was rebuilt after Confederate soldiers put it to the torch, along with twenty-seven other courthouses, to keep advancing Union forces from using the buildings during the Civil War. Paintings and photographs of former judges who had served this farming community looked down on the smallish courtroom.

There was a sense of history that morning as Tommy Pigage and his attorney walked to the defense table. Seated in the audi-

ence were Elizabeth and Frank, along with Rose Wyatt. A small
buzz of voices filled the room as the three awaited Judge White.

"All rise." The bailiff announced the approaching judge.

The hubbub of voice was replaced by shifting feet, then silence as the judge entered. Judge White walked in to take a seat
behind his massive bench. He shuffled his papers in silence before looking up. He spotted the Morrises toward the back of the
audience.

Good, they're here. He was not surprised by their presence.
This was the payoff of more than two years. He would have been
more surprised had they not been there.

"For two years the courts have been trying to mete out justice
that would be fair and still serve the goals of punishment for the
lawbreaker and satisfaction for the family," Judge White began.
"It is an impossible goal. Short of the death penalty, the family
may not believe the punishment to be just."

The Morrises winced. While that was true, hearing it spoken in
public had a sting that surprised them.

"The grand jury has already ruled that such a charge would be
too extreme by reducing the original charge from murder to manslaughter," he added.

Turning his attention to Tommy, the judge continued, "The
special prosecution has asked that you be sentenced to ten years
in prison. Your attorney has asked for probation. I am inclined to
grant both," he said. Then the judge officially sentenced Tommy
to ten years in the penitentiary, suspended that sentence, and
ordered Tommy into probation.

Through blind rage, Frank heard Elizabeth gasp. After nearly
two years, that was it. Bitterness iced their hearts.

"Will there ever be any justice?" Frank whispered to Elizabeth.

"He didn't listen. He didn't agree with a word that Rose wrote him." Her words were halting, almost trancelike. Frank looked at her in alarm. Was she about to have a stroke or a heart attack? He had heard of such things happening when stress became unbearable.

Although Tommy knew the sentence would be light, he still was amazed that he would not spend one night in jail. *You just dodged the bullet,* he congratulated himself.

"There are some stipulations that are attached to probation," he said, his eyes boring into Tommy. "I want you to pay close attention. If you break just one of these, your probation will be revoked. You will go to prison, and you will serve the full ten-year term."

Tommy did not fail to notice the sinister emphasis on the word *will.*

"Is that clear?"

"Yes, sir." Tommy nodded his head to emphasize his understanding. *What now?* He felt alarm sweeping away his exhilaration.

The judge began to read a list.

- Pigage must spend every other weekend in jail for a period not to exceed six months' accumulated time during the coming two years.
- Pigage must pass a breathalyzer test every time he entered jail for his weekend stint.
- Pigage must attend weekly meetings of Alcoholics Anonymous and supply the probation officer with proof of attendance.
- Pigage must attend alcohol abuse counseling at the request of the court or mental health center.

- Pigage must obtain and keep suitable employment during the terms of probation.
- Pigage must observe a curfew from 7:00 P.M. until 7:00 A.M. for 10 days beginning December 23, the night Ted was injured, for the next five years.

As each stipulation was read, Frank and Elizabeth felt their depression shredded by joy. It was a unique moment: one second, total dejection, the next, elation.

- Pigage must ride with an emergency ambulance crew to see firsthand the results of drunk driving.
- Pigage must work weekends in the hospital emergency room during Christmas holiday season or ride with ambulance crews during the holiday season for a total of 120 hours community service.
- For ten years he must send a donation of at least one dollar to the scholarship in Ted Morris's name at David Lipscomb College, and it must be on the anniversary of Ted's death.
- Pigage must write a 1,000-word essay on ''What effect my sentence has had on my future decision of whether to drink and drive.''
- Pigage must participate in MADD-sponsored seminars as a featured speaker. ''You will make six public appearances in area schools during your five years' probation.''
- Pigage must pay a supervision fee of $2,500 to the state general fund, the maximum fee, at the rate of $42 per month.
- Pigage must pay court costs.
- Pigage must take Antabuse, a drug designed to cause nausea when combined with alcohol, if the court or mental health center felt it was necessary.

And the most controversial ruling, which made national head-
lines:

- Pigage must attend an autopsy of a victim of a drunk driver.

"He is going to use every one of our suggestions," Elizabeth
whispered, squeezing Frank's hand.

"It's a small victory, but at least we've won one," he said,
putting his arm around his wife, his voice breaking. "At least we
won this."

But Elizabeth was not ready to give up her revenge. "Now we
have to make sure Tommy Pigage lives by the rules." It was a
grim commitment.

Saturday
October 27, 1984

Rose Jeffcoat Wyatt, vice-president of the local chapter of
MADD, had loved Ted Morris like a son. She had worked un-
ceasingly on MADD projects. Her mind had been a wellspring of
ideas, so it was not surprising that it was she who made the
suggestion that put the icing on the cake.

"I've got an idea," Rose began as soon as Elizabeth answered
the telephone early that morning. "The judged ordered Tommy
to speak at MADD functions. Why don't we make him speak at
Trigg County High School?"

It was a logical revenge; Ted had graduated from there only
two years before. There were still teachers and students who had
known him. The thought intrigued Elizabeth.

"I've already talked to the principal. We're going to put a
large slide picture of Ted on a screen behind Tommy Pigage as he

speaks. We've set a December fifth appearance . . . if that's all right with you," Rose continued.

All right with her! "I think it's genius," Elizabeth laughed. Sometimes revenge could be sweet.

"Let's make it the first meeting," Rose urged. "His first speech. It will be to students who knew Ted.

"I'll introduce him." Rose grinned at the thought of Pigage standing before an audience of Ted's friends.

It was obvious that this was not a spur-of-the-moment idea.

Elizabeth nodded her approval. A vision of Tommy Pigage squirming under a grueling inquisition made her smile.

BOOK IV
Rebirth

Monday
December 3, 1984

Elizabeth Morris looked at herself in the mirror. Once she had enjoyed dressing to go out; now it was a chore. She was painfully thin. Dark, almost grayish bands circled her eyes. A head of saucy black curls had given way to a rather plain hairdo, pulled back and cut straight at her shoulders. Wrinkles creased her dress.

She evaluated her appearance. *Drab.*

Well, you can't make a silk purse out of a sow's ear. She teased herself, but found little mirth in the popular retort. Once her hair would have been coiffured, every strand in place. Makeup would have been carefully applied. The slightest wrinkle would have been meticulously pressed from her dress. Although she was not happy with what she saw, somehow she could not reclaim her former pride. Life seemed to be a constant slide into even more depression. She could feel the presence of the twenty-two caliber pistol in the bedroom, where she had carefully hidden it from Frank. The thought of what she had nearly done a month before brought a fleeting shudder.

Is that a good sign? Had the thought of suicide brought the tremor? More important, did it mean that she now had more desire to live?

Doubtful! If so, then you would have given Frank the pistol and not kept it . . . just in case.

A touch of lipstick. Not too bright; she did not want to appear disrespectful of Ted's memory. She was afraid to smile, afraid to laugh at a joke.

Maybe I shouldn't go. All he's going to do is alibi his way out of it. All I'm going to do is get madder and madder. Maybe I'm starting to put my life back in order and seeing him will damage what little good I've done. But even as she debated with herself, she knew she would go. She could not stay away. Tommy Pigage's speech at the high school where her son graduated was a tiny measure of revenge for Ted's death. *So tiny that it almost doesn't count,* she thought, but she knew that she was going to drink deeply of its bittersweet consequences, no matter what the emotional cost. This was a milestone she was not going to miss.

Frank was pleasantly surprised when Elizabeth walked down the stairway. Except for church days, this was the best she had dressed in months. *She looks more like the old Elizabeth.*

"Are you sure you don't want to go with me?" she asked.

"Positive."

"It might help you."

"I have no interest in anything Tommy Pigage has to say," Frank stressed.

"I want to be there to hear how he weasels out of it," Elizabeth justified herself. "I want to look into his face when he lies."

She had seen a videotape called *Death in the Fast Lane* in which, it seemed to her, the speaker denied all responsibility for his actions by continuously calling the wreck "an accident." Although the tape was produced to be used as a tool against drunken driving, she found it grating. She was prepared to hear the same denials and excuses from Tommy Pigage, the same use of the word *accident.*

"You know, and I know, that he is going to place the blame on Ted," she stressed, changing her voice to a mocking tone. "He's going to say, 'It wasn't my fault. It was an accident. It could have happened to anybody.'

"That's what he's going to say, Frank," she added, walking to the window to look out for Rose Wyatt. "And I want to be there to look him in the face when he lies, when he says it is not his fault."

"Will you confront him?"

"I don't know what I'll do. I just know that I have to be there to hear him," she answered, a snap in her voice.

Frank recognized the underlying bitterness in her voice and understood it. Maybe this speech would be a catharsis for Elizabeth, something that would help her return to normal.

"There's Rose." She paused, still looking out the window. "Are you sure you don't want to go with us?"

"Like I said, Tommy Pigage doesn't have anything to say that I want to hear."

When she started out the door, Frank gently called her name. She turned. He studied her for a few seconds. "I love you," he said.

A smile—fleeting, appreciative, loving. "I love you, too."

Something was different about Elizabeth that morning. It was long moments before he realized Ted's senior ring had not been around her neck.

Tommy Pigage called probation officer Steve Tribble at 8:00 A.M. that morning. A fellow member of Alcoholics Anonymous had promised to give him a ride to Cadiz for his MADD speech, but had failed to show up.

All this before breakfast, thought a harassed Tribble.

Steve considered the situation. If anyone should be a practicing cynic, it would be Steve Tribble: He had heard every excuse. He had seen probation laws broken in such convoluted, creative manners that he marveled at the audacity; in most instances it would have been easier to abide by the terms of probation. Steve Tribble had been disappointed countless times, often by people he chose to trust, yet he enjoyed a resilient faith in the goodness of mankind and an instinctive desire to help troubled people who had become their own worst enemies. Often only Steve's intuitive belief sustained a probationer in times of crisis.

The school of hard knocks had taught Steve to probe beneath the sneaky wiles of the con artist, so it was natural for him to wonder if Tommy was trying to con him. Had he truly tried to get a ride?

As a probation officer, Steve knew that effective probation cannot be achieved unless the parolee learns responsibility while becoming self-sufficient. Steve had spent the better part of the previous week trying to force Tommy to be responsible for his own ride. When Tommy said his parents could not take him to the meeting, Steve suggested an AA acquaintance, and that appeared to have solved the problem. It would have been easier to let Tommy solve this new problem, but Steve feared the final outcome.

You leave him standing there, no ride, he breaks probation because he doesn't speak, and he's back in jail. Then what have you accomplished?

Nothing. But his logic told him that he could not do everything for these people; besides, he had an important meeting at mid-morning, just about the time Tommy was to speak.

All the more reason to get cracking, he told himself as he headed out the door, his breakfast of coffee and toast in hand. *I just can make it back if I leave now.*

Somehow Tommy was different. His soft voice, his hangdog attitude, his respectful demeanor all gave the appearance of someone who could change, given the right nudge.

Tommy may not realize this, but this is one of the most important days of his life, Steve thought. Plus there were the telephone calls. Sometimes Tommy called him every night to talk about his probation or to ask questions. All of Steve's instincts indicated that Tommy's life could be salvaged.

And you sure don't get many of those, he mused.

Tommy was standing at the curb when Steve arrived five minutes later. He crawled into the car, huddled against the door, and
looked out the window for the majority of the thirty-minute trip,
responding only to Steve's direct questions. Assuming that
Tommy was nervous about his first speech for MADD, Steve fell
quiet after a few minutes.

Let him think about it. There was silence the remainder of the
trip.

"Relax. You'll do okay," Steve reassured Tommy as they
arrived at the school.

"I'm really not a public speaker," Tommy said.

"You've told me that."

"I really don't want to do this," he said, as if expecting the
probation officer to change the rules. "This is the hardest thing
on my probation."

Was there a hint of panic? of tears?

"Get up there and tell it the best way you can," Steve suggested. "Just bare your soul. No one expects you to be a public
speaker," he added. "But, as you do these, they will get easier."

Tommy sat quietly, looking straight ahead. "Is she going to be
here?"

"I don't know."

"I'm really scared. It would be easier to take a beating than to
do this," Tommy complained as he got out of the car.

"I'm proud you're here," Steve told his charge.

Tommy turned to enter the building. Steve drove away, pleased
that he had taken the time to make the extra effort.

Jittery nerves were getting even more jangled as Elizabeth
helped Rose prepare for the program. The two had been joined by

Kentucky state trooper Stan Jones, who was another MADD guest that morning. The three were busy setting up a speaker's podium, slide projector, and chairs on the gymnasium floor in front of a rise of bleachers. Rose intended to make good on her pledge to project a large picture of Ted on a screen behind Tommy as he spoke. Elizabeth's gasp told her that the picture of Ted was in focus.

"When is he going to get here?" Elizabeth asked, a slight emphasis on the *he*.

"Any minute."

Their conversation wafted to the top of the bleachers, where Tommy had stood quietly for several minutes, watching the scene below. His heart pounded, his throat was dry, his palms sweaty. *I wish I had another drink.*

That morning Tommy had gulped down two bottles of beer. *It'll steady my nerves,* he had reasoned as he popped breath mints into his mouth in an attempt to mask the beer's distinctive odor. *I'll have to be careful that Steve doesn't smell it.* He had solved that by huddling to one side of the car, speaking only when necessary.

While watching the women at work, Tommy briefly considered running away. *Just turn tail and go. I wouldn't have to do this. I keep telling everyone it was an accident. I didn't do it on purpose. People just don't seem to understand that this can happen to anyone.*

It was an appealing thought. His predominant motive as an alcoholic was to flee through an alcoholic fog. It was refuge he would have sought that morning, except for fear. If he was caught drinking, he would be back in jail and then go to prison, and prison was his worst nightmare.

I just can't go to prison. Once someone goes to prison and gets out, his life isn't worth anything. He's been ruined, he thought, then he reassured himself and stoked his fears at the same time with the conclusion, *Most people feel that way.*

But there was something else, too. While preparing his speech, Tommy had felt a vague sense of duty. Was he beginning to accept responsibility for his actions or feeling a desire to help others? *Sure. You're standing here with your hands shaking, about to pass out from needing a drink, and you're going to help others? Get real!*

He studied Elizabeth Morris. Although his heart went out to her, her presence chilled him.

Why does she have to be here? Anything I say will be like rubbing salt in her wounds. This is the first time I have to do this, and she's here. She could have made it easier on me by staying away.

He silently cursed his bad luck. It was a touchy situation at best. With the Morris woman present, it became even more ticklish. *I sure could use a drink.*

"There he is," Rose whispered when she spotted Tommy. The words hissed across the gymnasium bleachers to where Tommy stood. Now that he had been seen, Tommy started walking down the bleachers.

"I can't stand to be here," Elizabeth said immediately, watching the man who killed her son come closer and closer. She could not take her eyes off him, yet she wanted to be as far away from him as possible. "This gymnasium isn't big enough for both of us."

Until now, Tommy had been a mystery figure at the front of a courtroom. She had mostly seen the back of his head. His appearance startled her. Branded in her mind was the picture of the freaked-out "punk" in the yearbook, with a mass of long, curly hair. This Tommy Pigage looked clean-cut, with short hair and a neatly trimmed mustache—not like the irresponsible killer of a young man.

"I'll handle it," Rose whispered to Elizabeth. "You stay here." She intercepted Tommy at the base of the bleachers.

What's she going to do? Elizabeth wondered.

Rose escorted Tommy the length of the gymnasium and disappeared into the foyer. After a few minutes she reappeared.

"What did you do with him?" Elizabeth asked.

Rose hesitated.

"Where is he?"

"I put him in a broom closet," Rose replied, amused despite the crackling emotional tension.

"In what?"

"A broom closet," Rose said again, matter-of-factly.

Elizabeth felt the hint of a grin flicker on her lips but she quickly subdued it. No matter how amusing the thought was, laughing would be disrespectful to Ted's memory. To find mirth in his killer would be dreadful.

"I didn't know what else to do," Rose reassured her friend. "I'm sure that's not the worst thing that's ever happened to Tommy Pigage."

Tommy was not sure of that. He sat in a straight-back chair quickly secured from the coach's office. The room was about jail-cell size. *It seems like everywhere I go I end up in jail . . . or jail of some sort.*

Janitorial equipment surrounded him. Mops, brooms, water pails added to the musty smell. At least there was the light supplied by a bare bulb, so he took out his speech to read over one more time. When she telephoned to set up the speech, Rose Wyatt had encouraged him to be blunt. She suggested four areas of concern: Tommy's life before the night Ted died; what happened the night Ted died; the fact that Ted's death was his fault; the consequences of his actions.

Steve Tribble had told him to speak from his heart. "Tell it like it is," Steve had said. "Don't put on a show. Don't try to con these people."

Tommy had no illusions of conning these teenagers. Some of them had actually known Ted Morris. It was going to be a tough group to approach and, in a rare moment of truth, Tommy knew that he would find no sympathy from these students. He feared speaking to them.

I can't wait to get out of here, get home, and have a drink.

Tommy sat in the broom closet on the verge of tears, his hands trembling, consternation eating at his soul, but he did find solace in the thought that he could find escape from his fears when he reached home.

Elizabeth was also wrestling with fear. At home it had been easy. In her fantasy, she would walk regally into the gymnasium, take her seat, and serenely stare into Pigage's face. He would speak. Afterward she would cut him to ribbons with well-rehearsed truths, revealing him to be the villain and liar that he was.

Now that the moment was at hand, it was not that easy. Elizabeth began to feel sick to her stomach. Bile rose in her throat as nausea swept over her. A headache pierced her eyes. She knew it was stress, but knowing that did not ease the symptoms.

"I can't stand to be this near him," Elizabeth whispered to Rose. "I've got to get out of here."

Rose understood. "Do you think you can drive? You can take my car. Go home. I'll call you when it's time to come get me."

The suggestion only brought dismay. *I can't do this. I can't go home. I owe it to myself. I owe to Ted!* "No, I can't go home," Elizabeth said. "I'll tough it out." *But I do have to get out of here.* "I'll be back when it's time."

She fled the gymnasium for the safety of an adjacent elementary school. Even this turned into an emotional nightmare. Ghosts were everywhere; Ted's memory saturated the area. Surely he had swung in the swing she touched or had drink from the water fountain she passed. Where on this sidewalk had he ripped that hole in his brand-new blue jeans?

Elizabeth made her way into the girls' lavatory, where she dabbed cool water on her face. Slowly the nausea began to subside as her runaway emotions calmed. *You've got to be decisive,* she scolded herself. *You may never get another chance like this, and you don't want to spend the rest of your life full of regret. Don't let him take anything else from you.*

When she looked in the mirror over the sink, she saw a tortured woman, but there was something in the eyes—a spark that had been missing since Ted had died.

I'm going to do whatever I have to do, she pledged.

A commotion in the hallway told her that classes were changing. It was time to go to the gymnasium. She felt her courage returning. She wanted to look Tommy Pigage in the eyes. No, she *had* to look him in the eyes.

With a new resolve she marched across the playground, her eyes locked on the door to the gymnasium. She had no time for ghosts. But when she reached the door a new wave of nausea caught her by surprise. Only sheer determination kept her from retching in front of the puzzled students who filed past her as she backed up against the wall, beads of sweat on her forehead.

"Isn't that Mrs. Morris?" she heard a female voice say.

Elizabeth failed to look up in time to see who it was.

It would sure be easier to go home.

With willpower that she never knew existed, Elizabeth forced herself to relax. The nausea eased. The more she relaxed, the stronger she felt and the more resolute she became.

She could hear the program starting inside. Only snatches and bits came through the door, incomplete sentences about drunken driving, statistics from Trooper Jones. Elizabeth edged to the door and peered in. It was dark inside. Rose was showing slides.

"I loved Ted Morris like my own son," Rose said as a slide of Ted came on the screen.

Elizabeth eased the door open, then quickly shut it as her stomach churned in protest.

I'm going to do this.

In a heartbeat, she opened the door and stepped in. It was done quickly, and that simple act renewed her sagging courage.

I'm ready, she marveled. *I'll take him on.*

Ted's face was still on the screen. The sight of her smiling son, her agitated state, and the trauma of being near Tommy Pigage took its toll as she felt her knees go weak. She stumbled to an aisle chair, settling into it with a sigh. She forced herself to focus on what Rose was saying as she wrapped up her introduction.

"I can't challenge you enough to remember that Tommy is going to tell you a true story. A story about someone many of you had known."

Tommy shuffled to the podium. Anyone else would have been a pathetic sight to tenderhearted Elizabeth. But he was a despicable killer brought to account for his actions.

Look up! she silently demanded, anger flooding her as Tommy stood with downcast eyes. *Look me in the eyes.* She wanted to scream it at him. To her surprise, she found herself standing, leaning forward, intent on making eye contact.

Softly, barely audibly, Tommy began to speak.

"My best friend, he killed himself from drinking and driving," he said, pausing as he moved his notes around the podium.
"There's already been one death since this program started this
morning. Every twenty-one minutes, somebody dies from drinking and driving," he continued. "One out of every five people
you pass on the street is drunk and driving a car.

"This is a story I'm going to tell you about my fatal accident
when I killed Ted Morris," he said.

*He admitted it! Right here, in front of all these students—in
front of me! He admitted killing Ted.* Although Tommy had already admitted killing Ted by pleading guilty in court, this ad-
mission was somehow more personal. Unbelieving, intrigued,
Elizabeth found herself settling back into the seat, tears blurring
the scene as she heard Tommy continue.

"It's something I'm never going to overcome.

"As Rose said, I got drunk on the twenty-third of December,
1982. I bought a fifth of liquor and went home from work and had
three or four drinks. I went to this one party and had a couple
more drinks. And when I left, I wasn't in a very good state of
mind. I was drunk and I didn't even think about driving, but I
was behind the wheel of a car. On my way home, I blacked out
because I was drunk, and I was driving a car. And I ran into Ted
Morris. It was my fault," he said.

It was my fault. She rolled the statement over in her mind,
savoring its sound. How she had longed to hear those words,
although she believed she never would. Now that she had heard
them, it was not justification she felt, but perplexity. Tommy was
proving to be an enigma.

"I went to the hospital after it all happened; my father carried
me home from the hospital about two o'clock in the morning. He

said the doctors didn't know if he would even survive the accident.

"Well, at that moment, it was like a ton of bricks fell on my back. I didn't know what to think," the repentant offender explained to his hushed teenage audience.

"I come from a fairly good family, but I'm just like the rest of you all. If you drink and drive, something's gonna happen to you, and it's not gonna be nice.

"The next morning, he was dead. I didn't know what to do. I didn't know how to forgive myself. I didn't know how I'd feel. Even to think of the anguish that his parents had gone through. I mean, this is their only child and he is dead, and it's all because I was drinking and I was driving," he said.

Our anguish? He mentioned our anguish. By now Elizabeth's amazement had turned into incredulity.

"I don't know even know how to speak or say or anything I could do to make them feel better. There's nothing I could do in the whole wide world."

He acts as if he cares how we felt. He acts as if he cares that Ted died. Difficult as it was for Elizabeth to believe, she summed up her emotions by thinking, *He's saying everything I did not expect to hear him say.*

"And I don't want to see you do it to yourself. And I know that the teenage group, it's very easy for you to fall in that bracket. 'Cause your friends say, 'Oh, come on. Let's go out and have a couple of beers.'

"I mean, I said it to myself. When that friend that killed himself was drinking and driving, I said, 'No. That would never happen to me.' The next thing you know, it's gonna happen to you.

"And I was just . . . ," Tommy searched for the right word.

"I'm lucky. Here I am out of prison. I should be locked up."

He's taking personal responsibility for Ted's death and admitting that he deserves punishment. Elizabeth did not believe that with everything she had endured the past two years, she could still be astonished, but Tommy continued to amaze her as he spoke. *Could I be wrong about him?* It was the first time that she ever allowed herself to consider Tommy as anything but evil.

"You might think that I have a tough probation, but I'll tell you what it's like. I have to go to jail every other weekend, spend a night in jail. I have to go to Alcoholics Anonymous once a week. I cannot associate with any type felon or convict. Must not! I'm gonna have to read these off, 'cause there's a long list of 'em.

"Number one. These are my rules of probation. Continued good behavior. If I do anything wrong, I could wind up in jail."

And I'm going to make sure you don't do anything wrong. It felt good to slip back into the old mantle of loathing.

"Two. Refrain from violating the law in any respect. That means getting a traffic ticket, reckless driving, shoplifting, anything you want to think about."

I don't understand why you still have a driver's license, Elizabeth retorted. It was a sensitive issue with her. Tommy had killed her son with an automobile, yet he could still drive.

Tommy listed the other conditions of his probation before noting: "That's a very light sentence. I was lucky.

"But there's nothing that's ever gonna change the way my life is from now on out. You can go ahead and drink and drive, but remember it may be your life or somebody else's that's taken."

It was a somber audience that filed out following Tommy's speech. Considering the topic, Principal August Pisa had requested that students dispense with normal protocol and not applaud at the end of Tommy's talk.

He did not look up one time. Elizabeth watched Tommy creep back to his seat. *Almost like a whipped puppy. Defenseless, morose, in need of kindness.*

Her heart went out to him. She did not want it to, but she could not help but respond to his hangdog attitude. *I have to talk to him.* She realized that more than two years of acute hatred could not be erased by a single brief speech, but somehow he had touched her heart. She did not understand it herself, but she wanted to meet Tommy face-to-face, only she realized it would not be the fantasy confrontation that had helped sustain her through the lonely months of mourning. Perhaps subconsciously, she wanted to nurture the scarcely reawakened feelings of compassion.

Quit trying to analyze yourself. You are what you are and you do what you do. At that moment Elizabeth faced two realities: She knew she would not rest until she met Tommy Pigage, and she knew that she was totally unprepared to deal with the situation as it had developed.

"What's the matter with you?" she whispered to herself. "This man killed your son."

I want to know if he's like this all the time or if this is just a show for this speech.

It unnerved her to realize that his contrite confession had cut through layers of hatred to the very core of her aching maternal instincts.

Tommy saw her approaching and looked for an escape route. *What do I do now?* Apprehension filled Tommy, who would not have been surprised by a physical confrontation. *What'll I do if she hits me? Nothing!* was his immediate thought, followed by, *I'm getting out of here.*

"Don't worry, Tommy," she called out as he started hurrying away.

Saying his name startled her. Until now he had been a half-human creature she had never thought of as having a first name.

"I'm not going to hurt you. I'm not going to slap you. I won't spit in your face."

He stopped, wary. He could not escape.

"I really appreciate what you said," Elizabeth started as she neared him. "You accepted the blame, and that helps me. And it will help others," she said, taking a seat and patting the chair next to her. "I know that admitting guilt may be hard for you, but you may be saving lives."

Tommy took the proffered seat, but kept turned to the side, saying nothing. *Boy, you are going to jail if she smells anything on your breath.* It had finally come to a meeting with the mother of the boy he had killed, and he did not know what to say, or what to do, except to keep her from smelling his breath.

That's odd, Elizabeth thought, *maybe he's too filled with shame now that he has come face-to-face with me.*

"I'm a member of MADD, and if you're going to be on these programs, our lives are going to cross," she continued. "Your being here has been very difficult for me."

Tommy was puzzled at the hint of compassion in her voice. Tears of frustration begin to ease down his cheeks. *I could sure use a drink.*

She paused. No reply. *Maybe this is as difficult on him as it is on me.* "We're going to have to try to be civil toward each other," she said.

Elizabeth noticed that he was crying. She pulled a tissue from her purse and offered it to him. The sight of the repentant killer touched her heart with leniency. Impulsively, she reached out to touch his arm. Instinctively, he turned at her comforting touch.

He saw a quizzical look. Her nose wrinkled slightly.

What's that smell? Elizabeth knew in a millisecond. *Alcohol!*

"Tommy. You've been drinking." It was an incredulous statement, soft, almost a whisper. Her hand dropped from his shoulder as if he had a contagious disease, the gentle face of reconciliation turned into an angry mask of hate.

"No."

"You've been drinking!" Louder, an accusation.

"No. No. It's cough medicine," he insisted. It was the only thing he could say, a familiar defense even if a lie.

"You know you're not supposed to drink?"

"Yes, I know." Tommy was contrite.

"You stood there and told those children all those things," she said, almost uncomprehending. "And you've been drinking."

"No," Tommy said again, pleading. "It's medicine."

Elizabeth ran to Trooper Jones, dramatically pointing at Tommy. "Arrest that man."

"Why?"

"He's been drinking. It violates his probation. Give him a breathalyzer test," she demanded, even more urgently.

"I smelled it on him when he came down front," Jones said. The lawman considered the situation, continuing, "I can't, Mrs. Morris. He has to either be driving or publicly drunk before I can give him a breathalyzer test." Gently, he added, "And he's not either of those right now."

Is this man always going to get away with breaking the law? An outward calm belied the hysteria throbbing inside her.

"I suggest you contact his probation officer," the trooper offered. "He'll know how to handle it."

"But . . . ," Elizabeth started to protest.

Trooper Jones held up his hand. "I'll take Tommy back to Hopkinsville, directly to Steve Tribble," he said. "You contact him."

It was not the solution she sought, but at least Tommy would still be in the presence of a lawman.

"Okay."

"Let's go, Pigage."

Tommy noticed the rough edge in the officer's voice.

Dejected, seething with anger, Elizabeth watched the pair leave. *What a fool I've been the past hour. Everything he said was designed to elicit sympathy.*

"I'm sorry, Elizabeth." Rose's voice interrupted her private thoughts.

"You shouldn't be sorry." Elizabeth turned to her friend.

"But if it hadn't been for my idea, you wouldn't have gone through this," Rose said.

"It was a wonderful idea, but Tommy Pigage ruined it," Elizabeth said. "And believe me, he'll pay for it."

Telephone calls from the principal's office failed to locate Steve Tribble. By the time the women reached Rose's home, Trooper Jones had already dropped Tommy off. Shaken by the morning's ordeal, the alcoholic young man immediately started drinking.

Meanwhile Rose and Elizabeth continued to try to reach Steve Tribble. Frustrated, Elizabeth placed a telephone call to special prosecutor Beth Myerscough.

"It's important that Steve Tribble doesn't think that he's got two hysterical women on his hands," Elizabeth had told Rose on the drive home. "It will not do us any good if he thinks we're just trying to get Tommy in trouble."

Her intuition proved correct when the probation officer finally returned Rose's urgent call after being called out of his meeting. He was flabbergasted at the news. "I'm not saying that you're not telling the truth," he said tactfully. "But I drove Tommy over there myself, and I didn't smell anything."

"Tell him to contact Stan Jones," Elizabeth whispered to Rose.

This is just unbelievable, Steve thought. *He must have smuggled something in before the speech. I sure didn't smell anything this morning.*

"I'll be back in contact," he told Rose as he swung into action. He left a message for Tommy, tried to contact Trooper Jones, and put in a telephone call to Judge White.

At 11:00 A.M. Tommy returned his call.

"No, I'm not drinking," he said at first, before admitting, "Well, I did have a couple of beers this morning before the speech. But I wasn't drunk."

Jones confirmed the women's report. "I thought I smelled something, but he definitely was not under the influence," he told Steve. "I felt that a breathalyzer test would border on harassment."

Both men knew that Jones had reacted properly, but it frustrated them to see probation restrictions sabotaged.

"I've got a suggestion," Steve began when Judge White returned his telephone call. "Why not change the probation to read that any officer can order a breathalyzer at any time?"

"Better still, make it any officer of the court." Judge White went Steve one better, extending the authorization to attorneys. With that, almost anyone could demand a breathalyzer on the slightest suspicion. "And failure to comply will be violation of probation."

"I'll get it drawn up and to you today," Steven replied. "Then I'll take it out to Tommy tomorrow."

"Good. I want this settled down as soon as possible," the judge concurred. In less than a month, this carefully prepared package may have started to unravel.

Steve called Tommy. After explaining the probationary change, Steve bluntly added: "That was a stupid thing you did today. I don't care if you needed to calm your nerves or whatever excuse you might want to offer. It was plain dumb. You do anything like this in the future, and you will definitely pack your bags," he warned.

Maybe a scare, a change in his probation will make some difference. Maybe this will help turn him around. Ever the optimist, Steve sought the silver lining after he hung up.

Frank raged at the thought of Tommy drinking and speaking to the students.

"After what he did. After killing someone in that condition, you would think he'd just run from it," he fumed after Elizabeth recounted the events of the day. "I would think that killing someone would have shocked him into never wanting to be around liquor again."

Tuesday
December 4, 1984

As Steve Tribble delivered the rewritten probation notice, Elizabeth found herself reliving the day before, examining every nuance of word, voice, and facial expression. Something special seemed to have blossomed that day, but she could not pinpoint it.

One thing I do know for sure is that Tommy Pigage is no one to fear. He's pathetic.

It was strange to think kindly toward him after two years of burning hatred.

Elizabeth went into Ted's room. She clasped the beach ball to her breast, closed her eyes, and fantasized driving down Tommy's street. But it was difficult to envision his death in her favorite daydream. To her surprise, she had no appetite for it that day.

"Oh, Ted. Am I being untrue to your memory?" she whispered. "How can I feel anything but hatred for someone who did that to you? to your dad and me?"

Her reverie was broken by the ringing telephone. It was Beth Myerscough, returning her call. Elizabeth briefly sketched the situation. "What I don't understand, Beth, is why he still has his driver's license," Elizabeth concluded. "He killed my son by driving and drinking, then he is released on probation, and he still has his driver's license."

"I'll do something about it," Beth promised.

No one can do anything about my agony, Elizabeth thought.

But you, came a thought that startled her.

Tommy Pigage stopped by a convenience store on his walk home after work. Some days he would buy beer and hide it under his coat. The walk to and from work was always difficult because he had no doubt that watchful, accusing eyes peered from each house as he passed by.

It would be difficult to determine who was more surprised, Elizabeth or Tommy, when she came roaring by him, slammed on the brakes, threw the car in reverse, and backed up to him.

"Get in the car," she demanded.

Tommy hesitated. *She's caught me.* Then resignation. *It doesn't matter. She's not going to leave me alone until I'm in prison.* Reluctantly he got into the car. It was almost an instant replay of the day before.

"I smell alcohol on your breath."

Tommy sighed. "It's cough medicine."

Elizabeth was silent, then she finally ordered, "Close your door."

"Where are you taking me?" The reality of the new probation order was all-consuming.

"I'm not taking you to jail," she said. "I just want to talk to you. I don't understand you. I don't understand myself. But Tommy, I need to talk to you. I need to understand what's happening." She put the car in gear and they drove off together.

"Why did you lie to me?" she asked. "Why yesterday, why today?"

"I didn't want to go to prison" was his simple reply. "If I did, you would see to it that I never got out."

His breath was sour with alcohol, but Elizabeth felt compelled to hear him out. "Are you that much afraid of me?"

"Yeah. I should be," he said, fumbling with a piece of paper in his shirt pocket. "Steve Tribble gave me this. Now anyone can order a breathalyzer."

"If I could have gotten one yesterday, you'd be in jail today," Elizabeth agreed.

"What do you want out of me?"

"What I want, you can't give back," she said softly before turning to him. "I wish I knew. For two years I wanted you dead."

Elizabeth saw him flinch. "Now I want you in prison," she continued. "I sure don't want you driving around and killing someone else," she added. "You certainly don't need your driver's license in your condition."

They drove in silence, meandering through the small town.

"Would you have driven home in that condition yesterday, if you had had a car?"

"Yes."

The word burned her heart like a hot iron. It took all her self-control to mask her resentment. It was almost unbearable to think that what had happened to her Ted could happen to another.

"How much are you drinking?" she asked.

"Since the accident?"

"Yes, since Ted died."

"Every day, after work. I cover the phone with a pillow and drink until bedtime—or I pass out," he explained. "But I always save about half an inch in the bottle for morning."

"Before breakfast?" She could not begin to understand this.

"It helps me get out of bed and to work."

"How much are you drinking?" Elizabeth was hearing things that previously had only come out of books or on the occasional television talk show she would watch. She had never talked to someone like Tommy.

"Ten, maybe twelve beers a night," he said. "Or a pint."

"Of liquor?"

"Yes, ma'am."

"How long have you been drinking?"

"Regularly?" A pause. "Since I was sixteen."

For the first time, Elizabeth heard Tommy's story, from his own lips. She learned of the grief he had brought his friends and family, a grief that compelled him to drink even more.

"If I'm sober, I can't take the shame and the guilt," he told her.

If there was ever a person who needs God, it's this boy, Elizabeth thought before adding aloud, "Tommy, you need some direction in your life. Would you mind if I sent you some Bible study material?"

"I'd like that." Tommy was eager to please.

"And you have to do one more thing for me," Elizabeth pushed. "I want you to call Rose Wyatt and apologize to her for drinking before the program yesterday," Elizabeth said as she parked in front of his apartment. "I could smell it on your breath, and Trooper Jones could. Don't you imagine that some of those students talking to you could smell it?"

"I promise," he said as she fished out a piece of paper from her purse and wrote a telephone number on it.

"Here's her number," she said, handing him the paper.

They fell silent.

"Tommy. You've got to do something about your drinking," she said.

"Will you promise not to drink any more tonight?" she asked.

"Yes," he said, wanting it to be true but knowing that he would take a drink as soon as he got into his apartment.

"I really can't explain why, but I'm willing to give this one more chance," Elizabeth said.

Tommy pulled his wallet from his back pocket and took out his driver's license. "Here," he said, offering it to her.

"What's that?"

"It's my driver's license. I don't deserve it. You can have it," he said, holding it out.

"I can't take that."

"You don't want me to drive. Without it, I can't drive."

"That's simple. Just don't drive while you're drinking," she said, slightly bewildered, ready to change the subject. Elizabeth wanted the license taken from him, but officially. *What good would it do for me to take it? All he has to do is say he lost it if he's arrested.*

"We're going to give this another chance, but if you do this again, I'm going to nail your hide to the wall. I'm going to be watching you, every move you make."

It was not a threat; it was a promise.

She actually cares, Tommy thought as he watched her drive away. As impossible as that was to believe, he believed it. *She actually cares about me.*

When Tommy entered his apartment, he walked straight to the coffee table where he had left his bottle that morning. He picked it up and poured a drink. He examined the amber liquid and its promise of escape.

I promised her. He set the drink on the table. *She just can't comprehend what an alcoholic has to contend with. It's something I can't overcome.*

The thought stunned him. During his month of treatment at VOLTA and the long sessions at Alcoholic Anonymous, he had paid lip service to the statement that he was an alcoholic, but now he realized the depths of his problem.

"I can quit anything I want to quit. I'm just not ready to quit," he had told fellow alcoholics at the AA meetings. The closest he came to truth was to admit one night, "I might belong here, but I sure don't want to be here."

Although alcohol consumed his life, Tommy wanted to be in charge. Admitting his problem made him feel weaker. He knew that the first of the twelve steps for a recovering alcoholic is to acknowledge a power higher than himself.

His resolve lasted an hour before he killed the drink in one long, thirsty swallow.

Wednesday
December 5, 1984

Steve Tribble was surprised by an early morning telephone call from Tommy Pigage.

"Elizabeth Morris came by last night. We talked for three hours," he said, detailing the events of the previous evening. "I called Rose Wyatt and apologized to her. Everything seems okay, now."

"See to it that everything remains okay," Steve challenged before hanging up.

I guess confession was good for him.

Thursday
December 6, 1984

Beth Myerscough expressed shock that Tommy still had his driver's license when she contacted Steve Tribble.

"If Tommy pulls another stunt like this, then we'll take action to revoke his driver's license for six months," she told the probation officer.

"I don't know if he will slip up again or not," Steve admitted. *But I'm sure he will, if the past is any indication.*

"We will be ready if he does," she said. "When is his next weekend in jail?"

Steve consulted Tommy's file. "This weekend."

For the third time Tommy prepared for a weekend in jail. The first had been a nightmare of cursing, sweaty inmates wrestling with each other, sometimes pushing and shoving. Tommy tried to stay out of harm's way, afraid to open his mouth. It was a night of emotional terror. *I'm as nervous as a long-tailed cat in a room full of rocking chairs.*

The second week he was placed in the drunk tank, removed from the people whom he considered wild, half-crazed outlaws. Since the jailers moved him away from the hardened criminals, the time behind bars was more of a nuisance than a threat. His concern was the nearly thirty-six hours without alcohol. He would go in at 8:00 A.M. Saturday morning and be released Sunday night. The solution? Stoke up on Friday. He drank heavily all day while loading trucks at the warehouse. That night he ate his only food of the day, a small bowl of soup, and fell exhausted into bed.

Saturday
December 8, 1984

The next morning, his first impulse was to reach for the bottle. *Not today. You've got a breathalyzer in a few minutes.*

He dressed slowly while battling slight nausea and an irritating headache. *I'm going to need a drink when I get back tomorrow night.*

Carefully he put the bottle on the kitchen cabinet, then placed a glass, mouth up, beside it.

Now it's ready.

Steve Tribble was surprised to hear Captain Paul Pullam on the telephone at eight o'clock that morning. "Tommy Pigage just blew a point twelve at 7:57," he said, getting right to the point. "That means he's legally drunk and in violation of driving laws, if he were behind the wheel of a car," he added. He realized that the probation officer understood that .10 was legally drunk according to the law, but he could not help but state the obvious when Tommy registered .12.

"Hold him for twenty minutes, then take another one," Steve instructed. *I want to be double sure before we do anything.*

*   *   *

Woman's intuition urged Elizabeth to telephone the police station shortly after eight o'clock. She knew that Tommy would take the breathalyzer test there, then walk a block to the county jail. For the first time since they had begun, she wanted to know how he had fared on the test that morning. The dispatcher put her on hold for what seemed like several minutes. When he returned, he was polite, but he refused to give Elizabeth any information.

"Something's going on, Frank," Elizabeth said upon hanging up. "I believe he failed the breathalyzer."

Frank smiled grimly. "Good. Maybe we'll finally get him in jail," he said, turning back to his morning newspaper with, "It's about time."

"He failed it again," Captain Pullam said when he called back. "He blew another point twelve."

"Take him to the jail and hold him—and hold the results of the test—until I can contact Judge White," Steve said.

From his home, an annoyed Judge White issued an order for a detainer, a legal document that would instruct the jailer to hold Tommy Pigage without bond. Steve would have to serve the document as soon as possible.

Tommy was whisked into an empty cell, number nine. He sat brooding until a jailer brought him a telephone.

He immediately called home. Phelps answered and listened patiently until Tommy had finished. He was unable to conceal his anger. "I guess you've just gone crazy," Phelps said.

Tommy asked to talk to his mother.

"I'm sorry for what's happened, Tommy," she said softly, but there was nothing she could offer during the brief conversation. "I'll come see you sometime."

Sometime? Tommy knew there was nothing that Judy and

Phelps could do for him. *At least they could have talked to me, make me feel better.* He had expected some type of comfort, but had received none.

It was the loneliest moment of his life. Tommy knew that he had just squandered his last chance. He had no doubt that there would be no other opportunity to redeem his troubled life.

You're just no good. The thought disturbed him. *What does that mean? People like me. I'm a good guy. Then why did your mother order you to leave?*

For the first time, Tommy faced the reality of his existence. He suffered from low self-esteem. He perceived that his self-loathing did not happen overnight but crept over him during the long months of drinking that slowly turned into years of self-abuse and cantankerous mistreatment of his loved ones. As he sank further and further into the bottle, he became more distant from his former friends, who finally turned their backs in disgust.

You are a pain to everyone.

Tommy knew that his drinking was destroying not only his relationship with friends and family, but also his physical condition. He drank such large quantities that he would become violently ill. Then the delirium tremens began—long nights of trembling, cold sweats, and sickening fantasies—and finally the blackout spells. It became easier to buy a bottle and sit in front of a television set and spend the evenings immersed in drink, alone. He had become too much of a burden, even for himself.

And now, more keenly than ever, he could perceive how his drinking was breaking his mother's heart.

I feel like the scum of the earth.

The thought startled him.

Why do I feel like the scum of the earth?

Because you are! his subconscious fired back. *Look at everything you've done. You've even killed someone.*

For months Tommy had acknowledged Ted's death, but this was the first time he admitted to himself that he was responsible for Ted's death. It had always been justified as the result of an accident or bad luck or a whimsy of fate. Never had it been the consequence of Tommy's drinking. He had vocalized a confession to his lawyer and in his speech to the students, but this was the first time that he admitted to himself that he had been responsible for a young man's death and that it could have been avoided had he not been drinking.

His drinking was not supposed to have led to death, but to emotional security. Tommy had discovered a release through alcohol at an early age. It offered comfort in an age of irritation, an escape in an age of discord, a golden glow in the harsh light of reality.

You found something that you liked and it separated you from reality, he told himself. *It made you feel good.*

But only for a little while, his inner voice shot back.

Now he faced the sober reality that in prison he might never have another drink.

Worse. You may never be free again.

Worse still. You may be homosexually raped.

Or you may be killed!

By now the latter seemed almost a relief considering all the alternatives he faced.

Lord, what do I do? he cried out in abject defeat. All his self-doubts and feelings of worthlessness crashed down on him. For the first time in his adult life, Tommy Pigage turned to his Creator for guidance.

Surely the same God that would spur Elizabeth Morris to talk to me can find enough pity to hear my cry, Tommy thought.

God, please forgive me for what I've done. I've ruined my whole life.

Tommy experienced relief, a sense of calm. He had finally sought help somewhere other than in a bottle.

Although he had made his peace with God, he still had to face man's justice. The chilling truth could be a long jail term.

Tommy had been given every chance, perhaps even more than most, Steve Tribble realized, but he had scorned every helping hand. Steve was not gentle with Tommy after reading the document to him.

"Does this mean prison?"

"I'm afraid it does. I told you last week that one more stunt and you might as well pack your bags," Steve said, an edge in his voice. "In light of what's happened, I wouldn't be surprised to see your probation revoked."

Tommy began to weep.

"I'm sorry for you, Tommy," Steve said. "I really am. You've been given not one, but two chances, and you've blown them both. I was rooting for you, but there's nothing I can do for you now," he added. Steve took a few steps and turned back, searching Tommy's face. "Why did you do this?" He had to ask.

Tommy was silent.

"You had everything going for you," Steve said, accusation in his voice.

Tommy watched Steve Tribble walk away. Steve was his last chance. His family had rejected him. Steve was too angry to try to do anything.

If anything can be done.

There was no one left, no one who cared. Tommy felt cut off from the world. Would he ever be free again?

You might as well forget it.

He heard a door slam. In a few minutes a jailer appeared with a bright orange one-piece jumpsuit. He tossed it through the bars and said, "Put this on and give me your clothes."

Tommy Pigage was finally a prisoner. As far as the law was concerned, Tommy was serving a ten-year sentence for the second-degree manslaughter of Ted Morris.

For the third time Captain Pullam called Steve Tribble, this time in midafternoon. "The Morrises telephoned. They want to know if I can give them the results of the breathalyzer."

"I don't think you should," Steve said.

Undaunted, the Morrises drove by the jail. Elizabeth knocked on the door. "Is Tommy Pigage in jail?"

"Yes, ma'am. He is."

Satisfied, the couple returned home. Frank could not hide his delight.

"Maybe someone's finally got him." He reached over and took his wife's hand. "Maybe we've finally got a little justice."

Elizabeth felt a stirring of vague uneasiness as they drove home. Tuesday's confrontation with Tommy kept creeping into her consciousness. She was haunted by the vision of a lonely, lost soul crying out for help. The events of Monday and Tuesday had so sharpened her understanding of her own motives—and her own unique needs—that for the first time in two years, her mind was crystal clear.

On the drive home that day, she was astonished to realize how much she had changed. *How will Frank ever understand what is happening to me?*

His hands trembled. His stomach heaved. He wept from pain and frustration. As midnight approached, Tommy Pigage had been thirty-six hours without alcohol.

It's not supposed to be this way. I should have been home hours ago.

He visualized the bottle on the cabinet, the glass carefully placed near it; both waiting for him.

I need a drink. I need a drink. I need a drink.

The phrase echoed through his mind, it became his only reality. And as midnight came and . . .

Monday
December 10, 1984

. . . passed, Tommy Pigage felt an unreasoning fear descend as he quaked in the darkness.

I've got to have a drink. He lay shaking on the bed, his violent shivering making it become a thing alive.

The rest of the night Tommy slithered through his own private hell as delirium tremens racked his body and an alcoholic craving consumed his every thought.

Steve sensed that Tommy was at the end of his legal rope. He could not forget the first time he had seen him after the guilty plea in October. Tommy's physical appearance gave the first impression that he was a street-tough guy. Five minutes into the interview, though, Steve saw a remorseful young man, obviously scared, and possessed with a good attitude.

But not good enough, he reminded himself. *He couldn't—or wouldn't—give up the drinking.*

His reverie was interrupted by his secretary. "There is a Mrs. Morris to see you," she said.

"I've been expecting you," he said after she had taken a seat. "Tommy did fail his breathalyzer. Tommy is now being held in jail and he will stay there until he has another hearing."

Why doesn't she react? He was puzzled. She finally had what she wanted. Her reaction was flat, not victorious.

"Eliz . . . , Mrs. Morris, there's something I've been thinking, about Tommy, and I'd like to tell you about it," he started.

"Elizabeth," she said.

"Thank you, Elizabeth." He paused. "The best way is to just get to the point. I think Tommy is trying to punish himself."

"How?"

"By drinking before he checked into the jail," he explained. "Think about it. If you really didn't want to go to jail, you wouldn't drink before taking a breathalyzer test—and you wouldn't show up at a MADD school program with alcohol on your breath."

The point struck home.

"He would not have done these things unless he subconsciously wanted to be caught," Steve added. "It's not just my idea. Some of the psychologists who have worked with him suggested it to me. Do you know anything about Tommy?" he asked.

"Very little," she acknowledged.

"He's only seen his biological father once. His mother divorced when he was very young. He's felt guilty all his life."

Steve held up his hand to stop the apparent question. "Don't ask me why. Who knows why a kid like this feels guilty, or why he drinks? He's been drinking since he was sixteen years old," Steve added. "His brothers are overachievers. They went on to get good jobs, and somehow I believe Tommy never felt that he measured up to what was expected. I've formed that conclusion because researching his life is part of what I do," Steve continued. "You know, and I know, that Tommy comes from a privileged family. He's not a New York street punk.

"He seems to have always been the black sheep of the family," Steve said before gently adding, "I wonder if you've ever considered that this family—this mother—now has to cope with the fact that her son is a killer.

"During the presentencing investigation I asked him about what happened the night Ted died. He told me, 'I don't know what happened. Somebody is dead, and I killed them,' " Steve stressed. "I think it's possible that he's trying to punish himself, and he's succeeded."

The more he talked, the more Elizabeth felt her compassion growing, until finally she held up her hand to stop Steve. "Has any of his family been to visit him?"

"Nope," Steve replied, shaking his head.

This is awful. There he is in jail and his own mother hasn't been to visit him. I wouldn't treat a dog that way, she thought, before her mind snapped back. *Wait a minute. How do you know she's not over there right now?*

"Can I visit him?" she blurted out, her hand darting to her mouth, almost as if trying to catch the words and put them back.

Did I say that?

Both sat in perplexed silence, each trying to evaluate Elizabeth's request.

Steve was as surprised as Elizabeth. "I could ask the judge," he said, giving her a quizzical look. He was not sure what he was trying to achieve when he started talking about Tommy, but he was sure this was not his goal. "This is such an unusual request, I think we should go through Judge White."

"Ask him, and then let me know what he says," Elizabeth said. "I'll go visit Tommy as soon as I can."

Elizabeth did not know that only family members were allowed to visit prisoners.

"Maybe you can go this afternoon," Steve offered.

"Whatever the judge says." *What have I gotten myself into?*
She was quaking mentally at the thought of going to the jail. It
was one thing to pound on the door and make sure Tommy was
an inmate; it was quite another to actually visit him there.

Strangely, the thought of Tommy punishing himself because
he believed the law had not provided adequate penalty made
Elizabeth feel guilty.

Cold turkey. That was the term Tommy had heard alcoholics use at AA meetings. It was always accompanied by a
tale of woeful mental and physical agony as the addict came
off alcohol without medication. On several occasions in the
past he had suffered briefly from delirium tremens, but it had
never gone this far. He had always found a buddy with a
bottle or managed to scrape up enough for a beer. *I understand
it now.*

It had been two and one-half days since Tommy had had a
drink. The desire was as strong as ever, a craving that consumed
him. His orange jumpsuit was soaked with sweat. He was un-
shaven, unkempt—an eyesore. His hands still trembled, but the
all-consuming fear brought on by the delirium tremens had begun
to vanish. He had eaten little food and slept only in fits and starts,
so his shivering body was weak. Bloodshot eyes looked out onto
a hostile world.

He did not realize it then, but it would be the last time he
would suffer the extended agony of delirium tremens. Tommy
Pigage had had his last drink.

O God, help me, he pleaded from the depths of his anguished
soul. It would be another long night of agony mingled with
prayer, but each day without drink became easier.

Tuesday
December 11, 1984

"She wants to see him?" Judge White mused after Steve told him about his meeting with Elizabeth. "What harm could that do?"

"Nothing, that I can see," Steve answered. "I just don't see Elizabeth Morris as someone out to harm him. She could have done that before he was in jail."

Judge White shrugged. "Sure. Why not? This has been one of the most unusual cases I've ever been involved in. We might as well play it out," he said. "Besides, if we can do anything to help that mother ease her burden, then we should do it."

Wednesday
December 12, 1984

"Rose, I've got to talk to someone," Elizabeth said late that afternoon on the telephone. "I've done something, and I don't know how to tell Frank."

Elizabeth explained her conversation the day before with Steve Tribble. He had just called her with permission to visit Tommy Pigage in jail. "I can't explain it, but I've just got to go see him," Elizabeth said. "I guess I think I can help him."

"Then you have to try," Rose encouraged her.

Elizabeth was concerned about the possible upheaval her visit with Tommy might cause her husband. She wanted to discuss it with Frank right then, but he was at work, making deliveries in the countryside. She would not see him until later that night at Bible class at Southside Church of Christ.

This was a decision she had to make on her own. Once made, she feared that she had opened a seething cauldron that could emotionally sear them all; but some force was driving her to see Tommy.

Do it now. A few minutes later she found herself standing at the entrance to the jail in the back of the county courthouse.

"It's not visiting day, or visiting hours," the guard told her.

Let it go. Go on home. You tried. "But I was told that I could visit Tommy Pigage any time I wanted to visit him," Elizabeth responded, polite yet firm. "Judge White gave me permission."

"I'm sorry, ma'am, but we can't let you in," he said, just as polite, just as firm. She might know Judge White, but she was not on the visitors' list.

"Roosevelt." Elizabeth remembered Steve telling her that if there was any trouble, she should ask the guard to check with Roosevelt Jackson. "Check with him. He'll know about it."

The guard was gone only a few seconds before he returned to open the door. She signed in. Her purse was searched. A jailer escorted her to a hallway waiting area.

"Wait here."

The room was dingy. By Elizabeth's standards, it was filthy. A single bulb hung high in the room, which held only a desk, a table, and chairs. Heart pounding, she pulled a chair out and took a seat, putting her purse on the desk. She folded her hands and waited quietly, every nerve pulsating tension.

When told he had a visitor, Tommy's first inclination was to believe it was Elizabeth. *You're a fool. She wouldn't come see you.*

He knew it was not any member of his family. If it were not Elizabeth Morris, then it had to be someone in law enforcement. *Maybe Steve Tribble. Maybe he figured out some way for me to have a second chance.* His mind paused at that. *You mean a third chance.*

It had been four and one-half days since Tommy had had a drink, and as he walked to the room, Tommy found his mind clear. His shaking hands had steadied somewhat, it was the first time in years that he felt he could think rationally, although his body still desired strong drink. Tommy realized that he was strangely at ease.

Because my head is clear? he wondered.

It was an awkward moment for both of them. Tommy retrieved a chair and sat down opposite her. Neither spoke after a clumsy greeting. Tommy wanted her to lead the conversation.

Why did she come? It doesn't make sense to me.

Elizabeth shifted her purse. *Well, here we are. The mother of the dead boy, and the young man who killed him.* The thought unnerved her. She smoothed a wrinkle in her dress as she continued to fidget.

Why am I here? she asked herself, before immediately replying: *I don't really know. I have some vague sense of wanting to save him. Then say something!*

"How are you doing?" she asked. It seemed a safe way to start the conversation.

"Just fine," he answered.

Now what? she thought, scrambling for the next conversational tidbit.

"Do you need anything?"

"No, ma'am. Thank you."

He's afraid of jail, I remember him telling me that.

"Is anyone bothering you?"

"No. My cell seems to be okay. No one's done anything to me," he answered.

Although her presence defied logic, Tommy perceived that her concern was genuine. He did not understand how she could care about him, but he accepted her concern, basking in the knowledge that her interest was benevolent.

"What about the food. Is it good?"

"It's okay," he said.

"Would you like to take the Bible correspondence courses now?" she asked.

Tommy hesitated. At his apartment he had agreed to almost anything to stay out of jail. Now he was in jail, so why take the Bible courses? All his life he had considered churchgoing people to be boring. They appeared to have little zest for life.

At least that's the way it looked through the bottom of a bottle, he reminded himself. *What have you got to lose? If you refuse, she might not come back. Maybe it might even be the right thing to do.*

"Sure. Why not?" he told her.

"I'll have Frank prepare them, and I'll bring them tomorrow," Elizabeth said. She had another topic, but she was hesitant to approach it. "Your drinking . . . ," she started. "Tommy, you've got to quit drinking."

"I know." *But you just don't understand what it's like.* "I haven't had a drink since I've been in here," he offered.

"Do you have to spend the rest of your life in here so that you don't drink?" Elizabeth shot back, an edge in her voice.

"No, I don't. At least I hope not," he finally said.

"Alcohol has wiped out one life." Elizabeth leaned forward, speaking with an intensity that was both unsettling and piercing. "Please don't let it ruin yours, any more than it already has."

"Once, not too long after I killed Ted, I went to a clinic. I didn't drink for thirty days," he said, hoping that would help. "But when I came home I felt like the whole world was looking at me—the murderer. I had to walk past Henninger's. I knew they were watching through the window.

"I knew you hated me," he continued, marveling at how good it felt to tell this. "I'd never been in serious trouble before. I'm not trying to give you excuses, Mrs. Morris. I just couldn't handle everything. I've wreaked havoc on anything or anyone around me. I've tried to stop, but. . . ." He looked at her, shrugged his shoulders, and lifted his hands, palms up. What he was trying to tell her was so deep that he could not articulate it.

"Then you will," she said, offering him her own resolution and strength. She had no idea of the withdrawal Tommy had just endured. "God can help you stop. And I'll be here for you, too."

Tommy realized it was impossible for her to understand the pangs of addiction. He decided not to even try to explain it. The fact that she cared had to be enough. That fact, and her emotional support, would be the strength he needed to remain off alcohol. *And don't forget God.* It was something he would have to remind himself of, over and over, until finally the Creator would become an intricate part of his life.

"You once asked me what I wanted. I believe I know now," Elizabeth added.

Tommy waited in anticipation.

"I just want you to know that somebody cares about you, Tommy." She found it easier and easier to use his name. *How do I say this?* she thought when he looked at her. Straight out, simply. After all, it is simple. *So simple it's taken you two years to reach this point.* She half smiled at the irony.

Tommy did not know how to take the half smile. He shifted uneasily.

"No," she quickly added when she noticed his discomfort. "No. Tommy, I have something very important to say."

She was in a quandary. It was her belief that if someone asks for forgiveness, you have to forgive, if you want God to forgive

your sins. She also believed that there can be no forgiveness
unless the offender asks the one offended for forgiveness. And if
there was anything Elizabeth Morris wanted at that very intense
moment in her life, it was to forgive. To her astonishment, she
also realized that she needed to be forgiven.

"Tommy, you know—"

"Mrs. Morris, I'm so sorry," he interrupted, the words coming out so fast they sounded almost like one syllable. "I'm sorry
I killed Ted. I cried all day when I learned he was dead.

"Would you please forgive me?" he begged.

Elizabeth's heart felt like bursting from the emotional storm
that lashed her. Finally, the words she wanted to hear.

"Forgive you? You know that when someone asks forgiveness, it must be given," she began.

"You? Would you forgive me for what I've done?" Tommy
was incredulous.

Elizabeth studied this young man. He had been an object of
loathing and hatred. Pick an emotion, and she had experienced it.

I hope I can, she thought, but she turned to Tommy. "Yes, I
forgive you. But, Tommy, you must forgive yourself as well."

"I will."

Elizabeth reached across to squeeze Tommy's arm. It was an
awkward moment. "Now you have to forgive me."

Tommy was thunderstruck. *Me, forgive her?*

"F-forgive you. Why?"

"For all the vile hatred I've carried in my heart," she said.
"Forgive me for hating you."

"I can't blame you for that." He knew he would have felt the
same way. "I killed your only son."

"I wanted to kill you," she continued. "Tommy, I lay awake
at night and considered now to kill you. I daydreamed that I

would run you down with an automobile and you would die screaming," she said. "It was not an idle wish."

Tears welled into his eyes. "I really can't blame you for wanting to kill me," he said gently. "I'd feel the same way if it had been my child."

As the man responsible for her torment, he felt a sympathy for her suffering that he never realized he possessed. For the first time, he felt a portion of her pain, a tiny bit of personal loss at the death of the young man he had killed.

Since Ted's death, he had felt sorry for her, even remorseful, but he never felt the pain of empathy. His total concentration had been on what he considered to be his bad luck.

She really cares. It was a wonder to him that she could. It was his opinion that even his own family had abandoned him, since no one had been to visit him. *How can she care, after what I've done?*

"You have to forgive me for blindly wanting vengeance, for wanting you in prison, for wanting you dead," she said, going on to explain her dreams and fantasies, which ended with him pinned to a telephone pole.

"All I could think of was my own grief. All I could think of was my son lying cold in his grave. All I could think of is that it should be you lying there instead of him," she concluded. "For that—for all these things—I need forgiveness."

"I do," he said quickly, eagerly. "Oh, Mrs. Morris, I do, just as you have forgiven me."

Lord, God, forgive me for my sins, for my hatred, Elizabeth silently prayed. And with that prayer came the first measure of peace she had known in nearly two years.

Driving to Bible class that evening, Elizabeth realized that she felt a sense of relief, because she had given and received forgiveness.

She wondered how she would ever tell Frank about the strange turn her life had taken.

She lay for long minutes after they went to bed. *How do I tell him?* "Frank . . . ," Elizabeth tentatively started. She felt him stir.

"What?"

She decided to wait until the next day. *When I've had time to think of just the right things to say.* "Nothing," she said.

It was difficult to go to sleep. She felt strangely calm, yet excited, and the comingling of the two emotions was not unpleasant. When sleep did overcome her, her tortured mind finally found rest.

In the Christian County jail, the emotional risk Tommy had taken finally hit him. *What if she had denied forgiveness?* This was followed by an even more interesting reflection: He realized that he had had no doubts that she would forgive him. When Tommy lay down on the small jail bunk, he offered a prayer of thanksgiving, then drifted into a peaceful sleep.

Thursday
December 13, 1984

When Tommy awoke the next morning, the first thing he did was offer another prayer of thanksgiving. The young man felt that he could never be thankful enough for Elizabeth Morris's changing attitude.

There is no way I'll ever deserve what she did yesterday, he prayed, *but Heavenly Father, I promise You that I will try to do something good with my life.* He knew that all the regret in the world could not bring her son back to life. He could not change the past, but he could do something about the present and the future. *I can do something right now.*

He believed that a door of opportunity had been opened for him and that he had been given a coveted third chance by the compassion of a grieving mother. Tommy clutched the telephone number Elizabeth had given him before she had left. It was his link to hope.

Frank had smelled the aroma in the garage. The fragrance of bubbling meat in spices and seasoned food warming on the burners had drifted down the hallway, through the den, and awaited his arrival. He smiled to himself. Both of them had been trying to watch their weight, but occasionally Elizabeth dished up a treat. It was a good sign. Life had started to return to normal.

"What's for dinner?" he called from the hallway.

"Humble pie."

"Who needs humbling?" he asked, giving her a hug and kiss in greeting.

"I do," she answered as he sat down at the kitchen table.

Puzzled, Frank asked, "What did you do?"

"I forgot how to love," she said, a hint of sadness in her voice.

"I can believe a lot of things, but not that—not you," he said. If she had not been so serious, he would have laughed at the idea.

"I did," she said emphatically.

Not knowing what to say, not even knowing the drift of the conversation, Frank was quiet. There was resolve in Elizabeth's attitude, so he waited for her to explain.

"I went to see him."

Instinctively, Frank knew the identity of *him*. His reaction was silence.

"I really can't explain it, but it was something I needed to do," she continued. *Why doesn't he say something?*

Frank studied his wife. For more than two years she had raged against Tommy Pigage. She had dreamed of killing him, had fantasied his death. *How many nights have I had to awaken her when she was having nightmares?* Perhaps even more so than if he had killed either of them, Tommy Pigage had done more to harm them than any person in the world.

"I went last night—and again today," she added.

He was confounded by what Elizabeth was saying. It was one thing to go to the MADD meeting at which he spoke. It was a measure of her revenge. Talking to him after the MADD speech was a stretch, but Elizabeth was charitable. It seemed within her personality to seek more information, especially after what she had heard. And going over to his apartment the next day. He could sympathize with her actions. After what Tommy had said, and after discovering he had been drinking, Frank suspected that had he been in Elizabeth's situation, he would have gone over with an ax handle to make sure he never lied again.

Most of all, though, it had hurt too much to think about Tommy roaming free and his son, unmoving, cold, the laughter gone. Frank fought back the tears. It was the first time he had felt like crying in months. The suffering father had found refuge in disregarding the past and living one day at a time. He resented Tommy's intrusion into his private realm of grief. It always had been easier to hate his son's killer.

Bewildered, he just stared at Elizabeth.

What do I say? If she wants to go see him, I guess that's her right. I know I don't want to see him. He's the last person I want anything to do with.

Sensing that Frank was not going to say anything, Elizabeth

decided to continue. "I went to see Tommy because I don't want it on my conscience that he continues to drink," she paused. "Per—perhaps because of us. I know we're not the reason he started drinking," she quickly added. "But drinking has already wiped out one very special life," she stressed.

We both know that's a true statement, Frank thought.

"I don't want to see Tommy waste his, too."

Ted never would have wasted his life. Tommy has already wasted his, so why not let him finish the job? Frank reflected.

Elizabeth found herself in an awkward position that almost cast her as Tommy's defender.

No, I'm not defending him, she thought. *I'm trying to save his life . . . and maybe ours.*

She knew that the abandoned Pigage would continue to drink and, perhaps, kill again. She knew that he would walk out the prison doors and straight through the doors of a liquor store.

He needed help desperately; just as badly, she realized, as she needed someone to mother. Fervently she pleaded with Frank: "The hate and the bitterness I am feeling is destroying me. I needed to forgive Tommy to save myself."

Elizabeth paused before adding, "And I need you to understand. To understand me. What I need, what my soul needs."

She's beautiful. Her soul's beautiful. She's the most loving person I've ever known. Inner rage at Tommy Pigage clashed with Frank's devotion to Elizabeth. The memory of Ted, stripped to his shorts, lying on the hospital gurney and fighting for his life, was seared into his memory, and at times like this it would leap back to life. His stomach churned as again he heard Dr. Campbell say, "He can't hear you." In the background, a man's sullen curses and shouts intruded into his concern for his son. He remembered what a drunken Tommy Pigage was like. *God, I don't*

know how I would have lived these past two years without her.
How can I refuse her? If she had seen Tommy then, in the hos-
pital, maybe she would feel differently.

Finally he spoke. "I don't want you to go down there. Your
soul is not in danger. His is."

Elizabeth was prepared for his response. "Do you remember,
during those early days when I wrestled with questions? When I
wanted to know why me and what I had done that God would
punish me?" She waited for his nod. "Well, you taught me that
it was not God that killed an eighteen-year-old boy. You said it
was the work of the devil. Frank, we both know that the misuse
of alcohol is a tool of the devil."

How do I say this without offending him? I would have been
offended a few days ago if someone had said it to me, she wondered. Then she decided, *Just say it!*

"Tommy isn't the devil." It came out firmly and gently. The
sound of the words seemed to echo in the room, foreign words
that seemed to hang in the air.

Frank looked up sharply, started to say something, but decided
against it.

"I know I've always thought he was the devil, but you were
right; Ted's death was the work of the devil," she added. "Tommy was his agent, but he is not the devil. I've me him now. He's
not what we always thought. He's different than we believed.
Frank, I believe he's sorry for what he did."

She could see this line of reasoning was making Frank over-
wrought. *Try a different tack.* "Alcohol has already wiped out
one very special life," Elizabeth said, a note of pleading in her
voice. "I don't want to see it waste Tommy's life, too."

She paused before adding, softly, "Maybe it's wiping out our
own lives, as well."

Frank looked at her. *She may have a point. Life has been a living hell for both of us since Ted died.*

"But still I can't understand why you'd want to do this," he said.

"Frank, I've tried to explain," she said tenderly. "There's nothing that can return Ted to us. But maybe, just maybe, we can return Tommy's life to him."

Each was quiet, lost in private thoughts. It was Frank who broke the silence. Although he did not understand her reasons for doing this, and although he refused to participate, Frank's love for Elizabeth won out. "I refuse to make this an issue in our marriage or an argument in our life. We've had to deal with enough, and Tommy Pigage will never cause dissent between us. You do what you believe you have to do."

"Will you go with me?"

"No! I don't want to be anywhere near the boy that killed our son."

"Frank, he's like a little whipped puppy that needs love and care. . . ."

"And mothering?" he said softly.

Am I that transparent? Is that what I want to do?

"He's not like we had expected," she said lamely, his question going unanswered.

"No!" There was a finality in his voice that left no room for further discussion.

"Frank, I want you to hear me out," Elizabeth pressed on. "You told me that it was not God's will that Ted died. I've had to fight to believe that, but I do believe it, now.

"It might have taken me a while, but in the past few days I believe I have come to understand some things that I didn't understand," she continued. "I'm not some rotten human that

God is punishing. I'm a victim of Satan, and instead of fighting Satan, I let depression and hate nearly defeat me. I was letting my life slip away. I couldn't concentrate, I couldn't think. I couldn't even function in a normal manner. I wasn't fighting Satan, and I was slipping away from God.''

Elizabeth felt the flush of resolve. She had set her course and was determined to follow it. What she wanted more than anything in the world was for Frank to join her.

"I need your help now, more than I ever have, but I'll do whatever I have to do," she said quietly. "Would you help me get the Bible correspondence courses for Tommy?" she asked.

"Of course," he said gently, but with a mental retort, *How can I refuse anything that has to do with things religious?*

"I took him the first one today, and I bought him a Bible to study with," she explained.

"Sure. Everyone gets religion in jail." He was surprised that his bitterness would extend into the realm of spirituality.

Frank had never realized that it did, until this moment. He had been the one to sustain Elizabeth during those early days by searching the Scriptures concerning the spiritual side of eternity; he had guided their study. How many times had he held her, reassuring her—and himself in the process—that they would be reunited with Ted in the afterlife, and that Ted would recognize them, and they him? These truths had brought him a measure of peace, even delight at the thought of reunion.

"All the answers are here," he had told her, holding up a Bible. The thought of a killer like Tommy Pigage leafing through those sacred pages chilled his soul. Somehow it seemed that God's holy Word would be defiled by his touch.

Wasn't Paul the Apostle a killer? Somehow that was different. *At least Paul wreaked havoc among early Christians because of*

*religious beliefs, not because he couldn't leave the bottle alone.
At least Paul believed he was serving God when he killed Christians.*

Frank's deliberations forced him to face a harsh reality. After
years of eagerly sharing biblical principles with a variety of
friends, after years of encouraging even the most casual of acquaintances to pick up the Bible—"All you have to do is read it,
it will tell you what to do," he had told them—Frank realized
that he could find no delight in the thought of Tommy Pigage
studying the Bible. Maybe he even felt a tinge of resentment that
Tommy would learn the plan of salvation.

Have I slipped that far? he challenged his innermost thoughts!
The answer shot instantly into his consciousness, *No! He killed
your son. Now he is conning your wife. And there is no room in
heaven for killers, liars, or con artists.* To Frank Morris, that was
the gospel truth, and he knew it was. Tommy Pigage could read
the Bible all he wanted to, but he was too far gone for it to do him
any good.

*I just can't understand why she will have anything to do with
him.*

**Friday
December 14, 1984**

As he had the day before, Tommy telephoned the Morris home.
His life became an open book to Ted's tormented mother. He had
no resentment at her probing questions. He found relief in pouring out his heart, which unleashed his guilt, and he assumed that
Elizabeth had found a balm he could not fathom. He had been
astonished that Wednesday night to discover the intensity of her
hatred. It was his belief that she had come to despise herself

because of her intense hatred for him. She had been impaled upon the dual dilemma of a human desire for revenge and a heavenly command to "love thy enemy." He believed that Elizabeth Morris needed relief just as much as he did, and the pair very carefully forged a relationship in these rambling, daily conversations.

Her first questions scrutinized those last few hours before the accident. She tried to learn everything that happened. But Tommy remembered very little, and there was nothing new to discover. Her questions turned to his childhood.

"Why do you drink?" she asked. To Elizabeth, alcoholism was simple: Either a person would drink or would not drink.

Tommy tried to explain to her what he did not understand himself. In later years he would come to realize that these conversations were therapeutic for him.

"It's like when I got into the car the night I killed Ted," he explained. "When you are under the influence, a person gets a strong feeling of deception. There is also self-denial."

"But I thought alcohol was permissive."

"No. I don't mean discipline, but self-denial through escape," he continued. "You think that the next drink will drive away the demons and soothe that feeling. Then when you sober up, the real truth starts eating at you again, so you drink to escape. It's typical for an alcoholic to think that if he can have just one drink, he'll be all right," he added.

Tommy did not know when he became an alcoholic, although he suspected it was when he turned sixteen. "I really wasn't crazy about it at first, but by the time I was in high school, I was using it for many things. Everyone did it, so I went with the crowd," he told Elizabeth.

Trips to wide-open Clarksville, Tennessee, started in his junior year. High school students were welcome in droves just across the state line, where the drinking age was eighteen and ID verification was rare. Tommy preferred riding with someone else.

"I didn't drive. I couldn't get a speeding ticket. And I could get as drunk as I wanted to," he said.

Although a starting fullback for the Hopkinsville football team, Tommy drank even more during his senior year. By then his grades had dropped from a B/C average to C/D.

"I was running around a lot. I was having a good time," he continued. "Alcohol helps you loosen up and have even a better time. You become more likable."

Then one morning Tommy awoke craving a drink. He discovered that his whole life revolved around getting that next drink. The handsome, All-American kid who played football, had a fine home, and had a future had turned into an alcoholic.

Elizabeth learned that Tommy had attempted to join the United States Air Force. He had started the paperwork in Atlanta and completed it in Nashville. Tommy had already spent several months on inactive duty and was awaiting a call to be sent to San Antonio, Texas, for basic training.

That day, and in later conversations, Elizabeth found herself talking about Ted. Tommy learned that Ted was in the Cub Scouts as a child and played Little League baseball. In junior high school, he joined the band.

Both could not help but compare the lives being discussed.

"What about your mother?" Elizabeth asked.

Tommy refused to blame her or his stepfather for his drinking, although his mother would later call the family dysfunctional.

"I did it. I'm the one responsible," Tommy told Elizabeth, before adding with grim wryness, "I don't recall either one of them throwing me down and making me drink."

"Who was the best friend you referred to in your speech?" Elizabeth asked.

A drinking buddy had died six years earlier. His friend had argued with another boy. When the other youth left, Tommy's friend started chasing him. He lost control of his automobile, which went off the road into a steel support wire on a telephone pole. The impact had thrown the hapless youth from the car. He was dead at the scene.

"Didn't it make any impression on you?" Elizabeth was incredulous at the turn of events.

"A little bit." Tommy paused. "But, Mrs. Morris, you have to understand that alcohol is very deceiving. It helped me believe that nothing like that would ever happen to me."

**Tuesday
December 18, 1984**

Another idiosyncratic development.

Judge Edwin White signed a work order that allowed Tommy Pigage to work at the tobacco warehouse during the day and return to his cell each night. Such orders had been issued for other prisoners during the month of December in years past. December is the busiest month for tobacco farmers who are working to process their crop and get it into the safety of the warehouse.

Steve Tribble studied the work order as he put it into Tommy's file. With the special visiting privileges granted Elizabeth Morris, he considered this case something almost out of *Alice in Wonderland. It gets curiouser and curiouser*.

This particular case involving the Morrises and Tommy Pigage was like thick molasses: It flowed over, around, and under what most officers of the court would consider normal circumstances.

Wednesday
December 19, 1984

It had only been two weeks, but it seemed he'd spent an eternity behind bars when Tommy stepped outside the jail.

You don't realize how much you take your freedom for granted until it's taken away. He knew it was unconventional, even a bit bizarre, for the judge to let him out of jail in Elizabeth's custody, but Tommy believed in the backwoods adage, "Don't look a gift horse in the mouth." He was just glad to be outside.

He was surprised to find Jimmy Hunter waiting with Elizabeth. Tommy vaguely remembered Jimmy from high school, but the two had not run in the same crowd.

"We're going somewhere special today," Elizabeth said when Tommy got into the car.

"Where?" When he had talked to Elizabeth on the telephone, she had only mentioned a speech to a Parent Teachers Association that evening.

"My house. I've made lunch for the three of us," she said. "Then I thought we might have a little Bible study before going on to the PTA meeting."

Tommy was silent.

Elizabeth could feel a slight tension building. *Maybe this wasn't a good idea.* She believed it would be best to keep him talking. "Frank says you're scoring high on the Bible correspondence courses," she offered.

"They're pretty interesting, and I'm learning things I never knew," he said. "Your description of God—the one in the correspondence courses—isn't what I've always believed."

"Really?" Elizabeth was puzzled.

"These courses show a loving God that I never knew,"

Tommy continued. "It's a God that I'm not so sure I understand. Basically, I've always had a big fear of God," he tried to explain. "That fear overwhelmed me as a child. It was an authoritative figure that was going to send me to hell if I did anything wrong in my life. If I'd do anything wrong, I'd be told that God knew it and would punish me," he went on. "I didn't have any understanding of a loving God, a sacrificial God who would let His own Son die."

The three rode in silence, each deep into his own thoughts, before Tommy spoke again.

"I never knew a Jesus Christ who said to do good to those who despitefully use you." There was an unspoken understanding that Tommy was referring to their situation.

The rest of the thirty-minute drive was devoted to the concept of a loving God who would only reluctantly punish in the final day, and then only because it was just.

"Is Mr. Morris here?" Tommy asked when they arrived. He knew it would be just as difficult to meet Frank the first time as it had been to meet Elizabeth. *You've met one and didn't get punched in the nose, but what about the other one?* Even as he thought it, he knew there was no physical danger, but his first meeting with Elizabeth remained vivid. Meeting Frank was going to be uncomfortable—difficult, at best.

"No. He's not ready, yet," she said. "But, he will. We just have to give him time."

At first, Frank resisted her plan. The thought of Tommy Pigage walking in his home was repugnant. He also feared for her safety. *Sometimes Elizabeth is just too trusting.*

"How about Jimmy Hunter?" he had said, "Take him with you. I'm still not too happy with it, but with Jimmy there, you can do what you have to do."

When he got out of the car, Tommy could feel the essence of Ted Morris. He knew that no matter where he stepped, Ted had stepped there; no matter what he touched, Ted had touched it. Ted's presence was everywhere, especially in the hallway where Elizabeth had arranged a photo gallery of her dead son. They lingered in front of the photographs of Ted as a Cub Scout, in Little League uniform, with the high school basketball team, dressed for graduation, even photographs of his eighteenth birthday party that Elizabeth had discovered undeveloped in a camera after Ted's death.

She pointed to a shadow box containing artificial yellow roses. It was nestled among the pictures and seemed out of place, a joyful yellow splash of color. "Ted gave me these. When I die, I want them taken out and buried with me."

A chill caressed Tommy as he stood in the presence of death past and death future. He was filled with a remorse that defied description. *This was a close family, and I created a great loss in their life.*

"Lunch is ready," she said, leading Tommy and Jimmy into the kitchen.

Tommy went to take a seat at the table when Elizabeth stopped him. "Not there. Over here." She tried to keep her voice from showing strain.

Puzzled, Tommy complied. It would be months before he learned that he had nearly taken Ted's chair.

"Why did you bring me here?" Tommy asked as they ate in the kitchen.

"I guess I wanted you to come to know Ted," she answered simply. "And I thought it might be nice for you and Jimmy to renew your acquaintance. Other than that, I really don't know."

"Your home is beautiful," Tommy said. He had already noted a lack of Christmas decorations in the spotless home.

"You should have seen it several years ago," Elizabeth said. "I was a much better housekeeper then, and I always decorated for Christmas."

"We had a New Year's Eve party here a couple of years ago. Everyone from church was here," Jimmy volunteered.

"How about a tour of the house?" Elizabeth asked. She led the men into the basement, which contained a pool table and video games.

"Ted whipped me many times at that pool table." Jimmy chuckled.

Tommy tried to visualize Ted in this home. He tried to visualize him surrounded by friends, laughing and happy, trading quips with Jimmy Hunter. But since he had never known him, it was difficult. He had no idea how Ted moved or his speech patterns or his personality traits.

Elizabeth ended the tour outside a closed door in the hallway. Without a word, she pushed it open.

"Ted's room," she said, stepping into it while Jimmy hung back.

Tommy stood at the doorway, surveying the room. Plastic dry-cleaner covers enveloped most of Ted's possessions: a television set, bookcase, anything that could collect dust.

"I've left it just as it was when he left," she said.

Shocked, Tommy felt as if he were violating someone's privacy. Seeing the remains of Ted's life was heartrending. He had heard of people losing loved ones, but he had always assumed that after a period of time the mourners went on with their lives.

She doesn't want to touch anything. She's afraid if she moves even a pencil, then it won't be the way he had touched it last. His mind raced as his eyes darted around the room before falling on the bed, which had been stripped.

"I took them off the bed a year ago," she said, sensing his question. "I put them in garbage bags and put them away."

She started going around the room, giving the history of each item as Tommy began to relax. He spied the beach ball and reached for it.

"Don't . . . ," a horrified Elizabeth started, but by then he was holding it. Quickly Tommy started to put it down.

"No. No, it's okay," she said, a slight smile on her lips, happy that she could accept Tommy holding the beach ball.

"Ted blew that beach ball up before he died. I keep it because it holds his breath," she said.

Plomer Hunter could not believe his eyes. *This is strange. This is unbelievable. This is the strangest thing I've ever seen.* Each thought became more incredulous, until finally he took the proffered hand.

Do I say pleased to meet you? He decided to settle for something safer as he shook hands with Tommy Pigage. "I understand you and Elizabeth and Jimmy went to a PTA meeting tonight," he said.

"Yes, sir," Tommy replied.

Elizabeth wanted Tommy to meet Plomer and Ruth before taking him back to jail that day, so she dropped by with her charge.

I never dreamed I'd see this man standing in my kitchen, Plomer thought. Strangely, he did not feel anger at Tommy. He was shocked, puzzled, and filled with one question: *Why? Why had Elizabeth done this?* Had it been him so offended, he would have avoided the killer and done his best to forget it.

"I guess Tommy didn't set out that night to get drunk and kill someone," he told Ruth after Elizabeth and Tommy had left. "If this helps Elizabeth, then I guess we can always hope for the best.''

Friday
December 21, 1984

Tommy's probation revocation hearing was set for January 10, according to a document Steve Tribble handed him that day on the job. Bleakly he realized that each day moved him closer to a final prison sentence, where there would be no work release.

I can't believe she can be so understanding. Judy's reaction to the developing relationship between Tommy and Elizabeth was unbelieving, but only for an instant. After all, more than a year before, Elizabeth Morris had told her they were people who bore no ill will toward her son. *If she can forgive Tommy, then maybe Tommy can forgive himself,* she thought. *God must have something special planned for him.*

Sunday
December 23, 1984

Floy Alverson was standing at the door when Elizabeth answered the chimes. It had been two years since Ted had been killed in the automobile accident. Elizabeth assumed that her mother had stopped by to pick her up for a trip to the cemetery.

"Mother, what a wonderful surprise," Elizabeth said. "I was going to come see you before we left." The previous year she and Frank had gone to Walt Disney World in Florida to allow their families to enjoy the holiday season, and they planned another trip this year.

"When you see us coming at this time of the year, what do you think?'' Frank had explained to his brother Robert, "I think it's better for everyone if we go away. It's difficult for us to get into the spirit of the season.''

They planned to leave the next morning, Christmas Eve day.

Mrs. Alverson came straight to the point. "I understand you've been seeing that Pigage boy," she said, an edge in her voice. "I understand he's even been in this house.''

"Yes, ma'am, I have. I've been teaching him the Bible . . . ,'' she started before her mother interrupted her.

"How can you do that?''

"Mama, you're supposed to learn to forgive and. . . .''

"But he killed your son, my grandson," Floy Alverson continued, remembering the bitter days that mother and daughter had spent at the grave site when raw earth covered Ted's coffin.

"I know,'' Elizabeth said. She did not want to grieve her elderly mother. Life had been difficult enough since Ted's death, with her father's long illness and death in June 1984. "Its . . . it's just something I have to do.''

"Well, there's something I have to do," her mother shot back in anger. "As long as you see that boy, as long as you spend time with the boy who killed my grandson, then I will never set foot in this house again. Not a house he walked in.''

"But, mother—,'' Elizabeth protested. There was no one there to hear it. Floy Alverson had already turned to stalk out of the house.

In a few minutes Frank found Elizabeth crying. He held her. He reassured her that her mother did not really mean it. They were words of anger, in the heat of passion.

"No, Frank. She meant it. Unless I never see Tommy again, she'll never set foot in my home.''

"It'll be okay. Wait and see," he reassured her while wondering, *Will Tommy Pigage ever quit dealing us misery?*

Wednesday
December 26, 1984

Attorney Jim Adams telephoned the Morrises in Florida. The lawsuit against the Andersons had been settled. They were instructed not to discuss the terms of the agreement.

Sunday
January 6, 1985

Refreshed, Frank and Elizabeth returned from Florida to try and resume a normal life.

Frank refused to forgive Tommy; his anger would not permit him to even consider it. Several nights he had had long mental debates over it, intellectual battles that left him exhausted the next day from lack of sleep. But most of his waking hours, he successfully pushed the thought of Tommy Pigage out of his mind.

Elizabeth plunged forward. Bible studies, baked goodies, and chats of discovery drew the hapless young man and grieving mother even closer.

As the days passed, her visits with Tommy established a ritual at home.

"You need to go see Tommy," Elizabeth would gently urge.

"I don't have any reason to see him," Frank would reply.

"If you would just go talk to him, I know it would help you," she said. "I know that we have always thought of him as a rotten degenerate, but he isn't. He is not necessarily more evil than other people; he is an alcoholic," she tried to explain.

"I have nothing to say to him," Frank would always end the conversations. "You do what you have to do."

Frank's permissive attitude and noncombative approach, coupled with her mother's refusal to enter her house, put Elizabeth on the horns of dilemma. *What if Tommy is only using me? What if he is conning me?*

She did not want to consider this painful possibility, but an honest consideration of her growing relationship with Tommy demanded that she do so. Also, all her instincts demanded that she believe he was true to his word. *But what if,* she considered, *what if he got out of jail and went back to drinking? What if he did it right now?*

The answer caused her to shudder. Elizabeth had become so emotionally involved in Tommy's future that she feared his failure might destroy her, too. She had given her friendship; she had given a portion of her love; more important, she had offered the healing forgiveness of Jesus Christ.

Now a new fear began to keep her awake at nights.

What if?

Monday
January 7, 1985

Although he was an accomplished speaker, it was rare for Frank to participate as a lecturer at anti-alcohol rallies, so it was with delight that Elizabeth learned he had accepted an invitation to speak on January 12 at the Providence Methodist Church in rural Todd County. His friends and business acquaintances on his UPS route were anxious to hear him.

"Why don't you ask Tommy to join you?" Elizabeth encouraged.

Patiently Frank gave his standard answer, "I have no desire, or need, to meet Tommy Pigage."

"But you two would make a dynamic team," she pressed. "The two of you would make such an impression on the young people there."

"No."

Thursday
January 10, 1985

Once again Tommy's court appearance was continued. It was déjà vu for the Morrises. Once again a long series of legal maneuverings took on the atmosphere of conspiracy as they awaited the final hearing that would finally put the man responsible for their son's death behind bars, where he belonged. Only this time, it was different for Elizabeth. What had once been an all-consuming passion for revenge had taken on tinges of conscience.

"Do you think Tommy would like to join us?"

Elizabeth had always believed this would happen, but she had come to view a meeting between Frank and Tommy as an event in the distant future. She knew it had not been a spur-of-the-moment question; Frank had spent many long hours wrestling with this proposition.

"Yes, I think he would. I'll ask him the next time I see him." She tried to keep her voice even, to treat it as a normal request. *Don't make too much of it. Once they meet, everything will be okay.* If he wanted to act as if his request was an everyday occurrence, then it was all right with her.

"Okay, do that. I think he will have an impact on the young people there," Frank said, breaking into her thoughts. "Just like you said."

"We'll have to pick him up early. There's a potluck supper before your talk," Elizabeth said, barely able to conceal her happiness.

Frank nodded. "I'm going to the gym to work out."

Friday
January 11, 1985

Steve Tribble telephoned Elizabeth. He reminded her that Tommy's probation hearing would be the coming Monday.

"I hope that the judge will not revoke Tommy's probation," he told her. "He seems to have made genuine progress since you've been visiting him. I don't know that justice would be served with him in jail."

"I never considered things religious," Tommy said as Elizabeth drove him to address a civic club.

"Unfortunately, most people don't," she said. Religion had become a common meeting ground. They could talk here without trampling upon wounds that still festered.

"I guess I'm not much different than most people," he nodded his agreement. "I don't think I consciously thought this, but it seemed that being a Christian was unimportant. All people die, and all people go to heaven," he explained.

"Sometimes it's difficult to look past this life," she said. "Ted's death made us look deeper than we ordinarily would have. We want to be with him again." She turned to Tommy. "And I want you there, too."

So do I, he thought.

"What made you live the life you lived?"

"I'm not sure. Well, maybe I am, but just don't want to admit it. I guess I lived for the moment," he said of his previous life. "I wanted the thrill of the moment, the escape. I wanted to do as I pleased, and when I thought about it, I just figured that you died and you went to heaven, no matter what you did. It was just some vague idea floating around out there that you didn't spend much time considering. I guess I wasn't much different than most people when it comes to religion and heaven. The past few weeks I've had plenty of time to consider."

"Not quite that easy, is it?" she asked. "There are realities that have to be faced. The Bible says there will be no place in heaven for liars, or. . . ."

Elizabeth hesitated. Had she worked herself into a corner? *No. I haven't. I'm not going to creep around the truth, and Tommy can't, either.*

". . . or murderers or drunks or adulterers. People like that. Sometimes I think that people believe the only people in hell will be a Hitler or a mass murderer."

Tommy laughed, appearing to take no notice of the list that included murderers and drunks. "I had never thought of it that way."

They drove in silence for a moment, and Elizabeth realized she had turned onto the highway that led past the cemetery.

"But something inside me told me something was wrong," Tommy said, breaking the silence. "My conscience kept trying to tell me that something isn't right. I believed in God, but only as an existence."

"He's much more than that," Elizabeth said. "He's a supreme being who can work in your life."

"I never considered my drinking something that would condemn me."

As Elizabeth approached the cemetery, she made a decision.

"This is where Ted is buried," she told Tommy. "I hate to drive by without stopping."

She did not have to ask his permission, but it seemed the right thing to do. "Do you mind if we stop?"

In an instant, Tommy felt his mouth go cotton dry. He could not have uttered a sound if he tried. He nodded his head in agreement while his mind screamed, *Not here. I'm not ready for this.*

"I won't be long," she said, parking the car at the Garden of Gethsemane sign. Tommy got out and leaned on the car door as he watched her walk to Ted's grave. She stooped and brushed her hand across the grave marker, her head bowed.

This is it. Now you really see what you've done. Something drew him closer. He walked to within a dozen feet of Ted's grave and stopped. Tommy could go no closer. The fear that had eased the day he prayed in the cell fell on him again, his heart pounding, adrenaline pumping so hard his muscles jumped. *God, I'm so sorry for what I did to her. She's forgiven me. Surely You can forgive me.*

Tommy realized that he had prayed. He had asked for forgiveness before, but over the past few weeks, he had grown to wonder if that was enough. Personal study, Bible classes, long talks with Elizabeth all came into focus as his mind raced toward a conclusion.

"Except a man be born of water and of the Spirit, he cannot enter into the kingdom of God." He remembered Elizabeth reading from John 3 to him during a Bible study in the bondsmens' cell. He had asked her what it meant. Following the teaching of her congregation in the Churches of Christ, she had explained that Christ was teaching baptism as entrance to His kingdom, and

His kingdom on earth was His church. That had made sense. It made even more sense when she turned to Acts 2:38, where Peter preached the first gospel sermon with a conclusion for sinners to repent and be baptized.

Boldly, he walked closer to Ted's grave. *I understand now.* But with that understanding came a chilling reality: *My soul is lost.*

Tommy did not wish to disturb Elizabeth, so he waited until she straightened.

"You can come closer," she said, her hand inviting him forward.

He shook his head no. Elizabeth understood, turning back to the grave.

"Elizabeth," he called out. She turned, quizzical.

"I am sure sorry that I have done this to you," he said.

She acknowledged his apology with a nod. She knew Ted could not hear these words, but somehow it was appropriate that they were spoken at his grave. There was nothing to say. After a few minutes they walked to the car and left.

"Tommy is not an uncaring, do-or-die, devil-may-care individual," Elizabeth told Frank that night after relating their visit to the cemetery.

They both knew she was trying to prepare Frank for his meeting with Tommy. What neither of them knew was that Tommy's excellent progress on the Bible correspondence courses, coupled with Elizabeth's gentle pressure, were beginning to have an impact on Frank. More and more during the long hours of driving on his route, Frank found himself considering Tommy Pigage's unique relationship with Elizabeth and, indirectly, with him. That relationship had led him to ask Tommy to accompany them when he spoke the next day, although Frank suspected Tommy might be a con artist.

"You're not sure if he's trying to con you or he really means to change," Frank came straight to the point. "His hearing is Monday, and he thinks that maybe, just maybe, you can help him."

Elizabeth did not deny it. She thought of Steve Tribble's call earlier that day. *Has Tommy conned everyone in Hopkinsville, or am I just a foolish woman?*

If Tommy was truly repentant, then her life would take on a whole new meaning.

Maybe Ted would not have died in vain. If Tommy turned himself around, became a Christian, and lived a righteous life, then some good could come from Ted's death. But Tommy did kill Ted, and there was no good in that. Frank had said it was the devil's work, and she believed him. If good came from this, then what was happening with Tommy could not be the work of the devil. It had to be the results of Romans 8:28, which declares, "And we know that all things work together for good to them that love God, to them who are the called according to his purpose."

I can live with that, she thought. There was special comfort in seeing the Lord's hand in the aftermath of the devil's work.

Saturday
January 12, 1985

The Morrises tried to treat this as any other Saturday, but as they busied themselves with routine chores, the lingering day was anything but routine.

Frank's first impulse was to leave Tommy standing at the curb when he looked up to see the neatly dressed young man carrying a Bible and walking toward them.

Oh, brother! he thought. *What have we got here? A jailbird carrying a Bible. Why did I do this stupid thing?*

He wished with all his heart that he had never thought of using Tommy at the teen lecture. All Frank wanted to do was leave and dismiss it as an error in judgment.

"It's not going to work," he whispered to Elizabeth, who gave him a quizzical look.

To Frank, the Bible Tommy carried looked like a movie prop, something that a criminal—especially a murderer—would carry around to change his image. *The tool of a con artist.*

"Look at him," he said, his voice acrid with scorn. "He's carrying a Bible. He's not going to con me. Maybe we'd better just skip it. Send him back in. I'll tell the people at Providence something," he said.

"Frank." Elizabeth did not have to say anything but his name.

"Okay," he nodded agreement to the unspoken communication. *It's my dumb idea; I have to ride it out.*

Elizabeth introduced them after Tommy got into the backseat. Tommy extended his hand. Reluctantly, Frank took it, but the touch filled him with revulsion. It was all he could do to keep from making a face and yanking his hand back. Tommy perceived the ill-concealed rejection, which added to the tense atmosphere. Each passing second seemed to make it even more uncomfortable for the two men.

"Tommy is doing wonderful work in his correspondence courses," Elizabeth said once they were under way.

I graded them. I should know.

"I . . . uh . . . I spend most of my nights working on them," Tommy offered. "I find them very interesting."

Silence again. Frank studied Tommy in the rearview mirror. Tommy was clean-cut. *Now!* Frank remembered the disheveled drunk in the hospital who would later claim he could not remember anything about the night Ted died. Frank could not relinquish the memory of the shaggy-haired punk in the yearbook.

Tommy's voice was soft, and his attitude courteous. *Now!* Frank could still hear the curses that fell from the lips of the loud drunk, curses that intruded into his thoughts as he hovered over his dying son.

Tommy sat with lowered head, his whole attitude one of depression. *He's almost like a whipped puppy.* The thought jolted him. *That's the way Elizabeth had described him.* Frank remembered an arrogant loudmouth pushing aside helping hands in the hospital.

He is alive and in the backseat of your automobile. Your son . . . . Frank looked across the hood of his automobile and remembered the matching metallic blue of Ted's casket.

Then Frank found the same safe ground that Elizabeth had used when she first approached Tommy in jail: biblical truths.

"Open that Bible, and let's use it," Frank commanded.

To Frank's surprise, his inward flash of anger gave way to his years of biblical teaching. There was always special joy in studying the Scriptures. *This boy may have killed my son, but he still has a soul.* That thought—almost a realization after two years of rejection—caught him by surprise. He understood now that perhaps part of his rejection of Tommy had been based on the distressing incidents at the hospital. What he had rejected for two years was the healing power that an omnipotent God can work through the application of gospel truth. Even with that flash of insight, Frank's hostility continued to try to block the spiritual illumination struggling to overcome his human resentment.

During the forty-five minutes it took to cover the twenty-five miles to the rural church, Frank kept the overhead light on in the car and called out Scriptures to Tommy, who looked them up. By the time they arrived at the church building, Frank was secretly impressed with Tommy's biblical knowledge. Not only had he correctly answered the questions on the Bible correspondence courses, but he had absorbed the knowledge.

However, Frank was still uncomfortable. Most of the adults attending this lecture were friends of long-standing from his UPS route, and he was concerned about their reaction to Tommy's identity. *You should have thought of that sooner.* The group had planned a potluck supper before the talk, and Frank decided to leave Tommy to himself. *I guess I'll just let this thing work itself out.*

Tommy went through the line alone. He took a seat at the end of the bench. Perhaps Tommy was even more uncomfortable than Frank. He found release in sitting to one side. *These people knew Ted. They're going to hate me.* Occasionally someone would stop to talk to him. What Tommy did not realize was that he was wrapped in anonymity.

After the meal, Frank set up the slide projector provided by MADD and gave a brief talk full of statistics pertaining to the county.

"Most of you know that Elizabeth and I lost a son when he was killed by a drunk driver who had had so much to drink he blacked out," Frank began. "It was a tragedy that I doubt Elizabeth or I will ever get over. Not a day goes by that I don't think of Ted. It's true that the intensity of your pain passes, but the pain itself never leaves. It is something that we will live with for the rest of our lives.

"We have with us tonight a young man who, also, will have

to live with Ted's death the rest of his life.'' He heard rustling in the audience as some began to understand the identity of the quiet young man. ''His name is Tommy Pigage.''

There was a gasp from the audience.

''He was driving the other car the night Ted died,'' Frank explained. ''I want to ask you to do me a favor. Please listen to Tommy. And as you listen, please consider what I just said. Like us, Tommy will always have to live with the memory of Ted's death.''

Tommy was surprised at the compassionate introduction. Because Frank had shunned him most of the night, he was prepared for the worst. Instead, his speech went well; his shy, soft-spoken approach had the audience's full attention until the end of his talk.

He's very effective. Frank approved of Tommy's honest presentation. *I can see why Elizabeth was so touched by him.*

''Those were nice people,'' Tommy ventured once the three started back to Hopkinsville. He was gratified that he had not been rejected.

''People want to know about you,'' Frank replied.

Tommy understood. He could tell by the questions, by the sidelong looks that people had difficulty correlating the soft-spoken, instinctively friendly manner with the image of a wild-eyed drunk who killed someone. *That was another person,* he thought. Tommy also realized that people who knew his background would have to alter their own predetermined concepts before accepting him as he now was. On the other hand, each new person he met would only meet the reformed Tommy Pigage. That thought pleased him. But he was restless in his soul. His life might be straightening out with mankind, but he knew that he still faced prison for what he had done. He would deal with that when it came. He had to pay the price for his actions.

What concerned Tommy now was his spiritual well-being. He had prayed. He had asked for forgiveness of his sins, but he had come to realize he had not fulfilled the requirements he had discovered in the Bible, requirements that would cleanse his soul.

"Mr. Morris, I want to be baptized," he said, leaning forward in the seat.

Frank was quiet for a few seconds. Tommy waited expectantly.

"Do you believe in God?"

"Yes, sir, I do," he said. "And Mr. Morris, I know that I'm a sinner. I killed your son, and that's a sin for sure."

Very carefully Frank guided Tommy through the examples of biblical salvation in the Book of Acts. As members of the Church of Christ, the Morrises believe the Bible teaches that forgiveness of sins occurs only with the act of baptism by immersion, which is a spiritual cleansing of all past sins. The immersion is a spiritual recreation of Christ's death, burial, and resurrection, and as Christ arose in a new body, so will the newborn Christian arise in a sinless state. Should Tommy take this step, then in God's eyes, all would be forgiven.

As they neared the Little River Church of Christ, Frank went over the five steps in the plan of salvation. Tommy had heard the gospel. He obviously believed it.

"Tommy, have you ever confessed that Jesus Christ is the Son of God?"

"I don't know, Mr. Morris. I've always believed in God, and in Christ," he said, pondering the question. "But I'll tell you both this right now. I believe that Jesus Christ is the Son of God, and I'll tell everyone I'll ever meet from now on."

Even in prison, he determined.

"On the day of Pentecost, Peter told the multitudes to repent and be baptized," Frank said, listing the last two steps.

"I've already repented. I'm so sorry for what I've done that I can barely live with myself," Tommy said. "Only Mrs. Morris's forgiving attitude has helped keep me going. Now I want God's forgiveness through baptism."

"I can baptize you right now," Frank said. "The church building is right up the road."

"I would really want that," was Tommy's trembling reply. Frank pulled into the parking lot that cold January night. Somberly they entered the building. Elizabeth took a seat in the front row.

Tommy and Frank went into the dressing room, where they donned white overalls. *It must be forty degrees in here,* Frank thought. "You'd better turn on the heater. I don't want you to catch cold," Frank said when he noticed Tommy shivering. The older man put on hip-high wading boots.

Elizabeth noticed the steam rising off the frigid water from their body heat when Frank and Tommy entered the baptistery. Tears of sorrow and joy mingled on her cheeks.

Sorrow. She relived the night an eleven-year-old boy made a conscious decision, just as Tommy had made his. Joy. A new soul was joining God's kingdom.

"Tommy, do you believe that Jesus Christ is the Son of God?"

"Yes, sir, I do."

Frank raised his hand in prayer. "According to the teachings of God's Holy Scripture, I now baptize you in the name of the Father, and the Son, and the Holy Spirit, for the remission of your sins."

Tommy was holding a handkerchief that Frank placed over his nose as he lowered him backward into the water until he was fully immersed.

"Amen," Frank whispered when he raised Tommy up.

"Amen," Elizabeth echoed.

"Amen," Tommy said with emphasis.

Tommy was reborn a new soul, now sinless because God had forgiven all his sins, including the killing of their son. In one of those ironies of life, the offended had performed the ritual that would cleanse the offender.

Unable to contain himself, Tommy threw his arms around Frank. "Can you forgive me?"

A clash of emotions shook Frank to his very soul. Later he would tell Elizabeth, "I didn't know that a man could have that many conflicting emotions at one time." He felt happiness, hate, love, and remorse. For seconds his body trembled. He remembered the night of the telephone call more than two years before, when Ted lay dying. At that time he believed he could kill Tommy. He remembered Elizabeth's threat to kill Tommy with her car. He recalled the intensity of his own hatred, so bitter that he could not even speak of it. He remembered Elizabeth's depression, her being adrift on a turbulent emotional sea. He relived the day Elizabeth told him she had nearly committed suicide. He was overwhelmed by his memory of Ted, his pride in his son, the sweetness of his youth, the joy of his teenage years. More than two years of loss and anguish crashed down on this man who had only wanted to love his family, be loved in turn, and eventually join them in a higher reward after death.

God, what do I do? Frank cried out mentally, and for the first time, he noticed that tears were running down his cheeks.

"Yes," Frank said, looking across at Elizabeth, who now stood by the baptistery, crying.

The words choked in his throat before tumbling out: "I forgive you."

You do what you have to do, he thought. He would have to

nurture that spirit of forgiveness, but he knew he could sustain it, because he, too, had had a change of attitude. *Somehow, I feel cleansed myself.*

That night three people who had found a measure of peace within themselves because they had found peace with God went home to begin a new life as friends and fellow Christians.

The Beginning

Epilogue

Two days after Tommy Pigage was baptized, he entered a plea of guilty for failing to refrain from the use of alcohol. Judge White revoked his probation, and Tommy was ordered to serve his original ten-year sentence. Tommy was to remain in county jail until his transfer to the state penitentiary, because there was no room to accommodate him in the state facility.

Frank and Elizabeth petitioned Judge White for continued visitation rights. Ted's parents would pick up Tommy at the jail each Sunday morning, and he would spend the day with them, returning to jail after Sunday evening worship services. Judge White also allowed Tommy to attend Wednesday evening Bible class with the Morrises.

The long Sundays in their home with Tommy called for a unique period of adjustment for all three. Each visit helped erase a portion of the old hatred and the old fear, as the three began to know and understand one another.

Not long after the probation was revoked, Judge White contacted the Morrises. In the State of Kentucky it is possible to reinstate probation if the criminal has shown marked improvement during a three-month period immediately following probation revocation.

The Morrises would not object to the judge entertaining such a move.

During his three-month jail stay, Tommy was attacked one night by an inmate intent on committing a sexual crime, one of the worst fears he had had upon entering jail. He successfully fought off the attacker.

On April 12, Tommy Pigage was brought to court fully expecting to leave the courthouse that day for a cell in the state penitentiary. Instead, he received a stern lecture from the judge after a hearing and was given "shock probation." Tommy was released under the terms of the previous probation that had been so carefully worked out by court officers and MADD.

Tommy went on to fulfill the stipulations of probation, with the exception of the most notorious one. He did not see an autopsy performed. Judge White tried to arrange Tommy's presence at an autopsy performed by the medical examiner in the local hospital, but authorities at the hospital would not allow it.

In 1986 Frank and Elizabeth decided to sell their country home and move into Hopkinsville. They would start anew. They could build new memories, although Ted's memory would remain a daily part of their lives. Ted's desk, still intact, was moved to the new home: most of his other possessions were stored. Elizabeth tenderly placed the still-inflated beach ball into one of the last boxes that was sealed and stored. She has not seen it since that day.

Tommy could no longer associate with his former friends, so

the Christian family at Little River Church of Christ rallied around him, offering a network of support.

Eventually, Jimmy Hunter introduced Tommy to a former college classmate. Romance soon blossomed. Tommy Pigage and Jacque Newby were married on November 6, 1987. Proud parents Phelps and Judy Anderson and Bill and Margie Newby attended the ceremony in the Morrises' new home. Judy came early and helped Elizabeth decorate the house for the happy occasion. Since all men in the Church of Christ are considered ministers, Frank performed the marriage ceremony.

Tommy and his new bride purchased a home on the same block as the Morrises. The couples vacation together each Christmas and often take trips during the summer.

"As Christians, Frank and Elizabeth have been able to overcome this great grief," Tommy says. "They've helped me fill an empty spot. I hope I've helped them."

Tommy's relationship with his mother and stepfather has never been better.

One day, not long after Tommy and Jackie married, Elizabeth decided that the time was right, so she went to the toy store in the mall, where she purchased the lifelike baby doll she had longed for and admired so many months ago.

Elizabeth paid dearly for practicing Christian forgiveness. True to her word, her mother never set foot in Elizabeth's home again before she died in 1985.

As this book was being written, the Morrises discovered why Tommy retained his driver's license: He was never charged with driving under the influence. Murder charges had been filed by dedicated police officers seeking the most drastic penalty possible. If misdemeanor DUI charges had been filed, then the felony murder case might have been compromised.

On April 12, 1990, Tommy Pigage petitioned for the return of
his civil rights, which had automatically been revoked when he
was found guilty of a felony. They have since been restored.

Although there has been forgiveness, there will always be a
memory and a campaign.

"We forgave our son's killer because it was right, but we do
not forget," Frank says. "We still believe that the stiffer the
penalties, the fewer drunk drivers there will be on our roads."

In the aftermath of Tommy's conversion, several people have
suggested that Ted gave his life for Tommy's salvation.

"Ted did not give his life," Frank is quick to point out. "It
was taken from him. And there is no way I would have ever
allowed Ted to die for anyone.

"Losing Ted did help us understand the reality of John 3:16,
and perhaps some of the heartache a loving God can have,"
Frank has explained. "We realize how precious a son is. If God
gave His only Son to die, then it is certainly easy to believe that
He wants mankind to take advantage of the sacrifice and be
saved."

With forgiveness has come a unique perspective that perhaps
only a handful of people will ever experience. Elizabeth believes
that she and Frank understand—within a finite human
framework—a portion of God's suffering when He allowed His
own Son to die for the sins of the world.

In a moving speech to a group of women at Freed-Hardeman
College, she said:

> Ted died, but something good has come from it.
> Ted's death was not our choice. Can you image the hurt,
> the pain that God must feel, after allowing his Son to die,
> for people to reject this sacrifice and live a sinful life? There

must be a special pain when people fall away who had once accepted Christianity.

I honestly don't know if I could stand it if Tommy returned to his former life.